FOR THE TABLE

FOR THE TABLE

EASY, ADAPTABLE, CROWD-PLEASING RECIPES

ANNA STOCKWELL

Photography by Chelsea Kyle

Abrams, New York

FOR ALL THE FRIENDS AND LOVERS WHO
HAVE FILLED THE SEATS AT MY TABLE,
WITH LOVE AND THANKS

CONTENTS

Introduction

This is a book for a new way of planning and cooking dinner menus that are simpler, more flexible, and more fun. It's here to prove that a dinner party doesn't need to be formal or fussy or even a lot of work to be celebratory and meaningful, and I'm here to teach you how.

I believe that the act of gathering around the table is what's actually special and most important about a dinner party. Putting out a couple platters of food prepared just for that table of people, and passing those platters around until everyone's had their fill—this sharing feeds more than just bellies. It is what helps us stay connected, form new relationships, and maintain lasting bonds with our chosen families. Now more than ever, this act of intentional gathering for a festive dinner is a useful ritual to bring into our lives. It's uplifting, it's fulfilling, and it's a lot of fun.

The menus that follow are each built around two large platters for the table. These are not the meat-and-three-sides dinners our grandparents or parents served. While one dish in each menu is often more protein-forward than the other, neither is necessarily the main. Instead, they costar, each giving a shining performance on its own, but together are a true showstopper. Many of the menus include meat, but I don't believe we should all be eating meat all the time—these are special occasion menus, and so I source my meat carefully from local organic farms and enjoy every bite of it. When meat is on the menus that follow, though, I always provide tips for how to feed a meat-free guest, and there are plenty of vegetarian menus too.

Making just two large-format recipes is my favorite way to host dinner for a crowd of any size and works just as well for your weeknight family dinners as it does for entertaining. When you focus on making just two special things for dinner, you can actually have time to bake a cake and change your clothes before dinner too, and everything you make is better for not being rushed in the hustle of too many things. In addition to making life easier, serving dinner family style lets everyone choose what ends up on their plates, and the passing of platters back and forth across the table (or the revisiting of platters on a buffet) creates connection among a group.

The two recipes that anchor each menu are designed to go together, and I hope you will try serving them together, but you can, of course, pick them apart and reconfigure as desired. My menus are organized by season because that's how I like to cook, and what I want to eat depends so much on weather and seasonal availability. So if you do mix and match recipes, it's best to do so within a season. In addition to a couple platters, I almost always add a sauce, because I've found that nothing more easily makes a dinner feel like a *special* dinner than serving a homemade sauce for the table. I've left the after-dinner sweet and before-dinner snack planning of the menu up to you though, with an arsenal of easy no- to low-cook snacks and gluten-free desserts that you can add to any menu.

I've been hosting dinner parties since I was a teenager (I even dabbled in it as a kid), and there is still nothing that makes me happier. Over the last decade plus, I've worked in the editorial offices and test kitchens of some of the best food magazines and websites, including *SAVEUR*, Epicurious, and *Bon Appétit*, and I got my culinary degree at the International Culinary Center in New York City in the process. As a food editor for Epicurious, I learned how to streamline and simplify my recipes as much as possible without sacrificing flavor to make them foolproof for home cooks, and developed more 30-minute weeknight dinners than I can count. I know that your time, dear reader, is precious, and I will never waste it. While working full-time and overtime in NYC food media, I kept hosting constantly, cooking in a small apartment kitchen with no dishwasher. My lack of time and kitchen space taught me how to focus on what really matters when entertaining, and how to streamline my cooking and prep as much food ahead as possible to minimize dishes and maximize my own enjoyment of my time with my guests. (I now live in the Hudson Valley with a bigger kitchen and a dishwasher, but I still like to cook and entertain this way.) The menus that follow almost all appeared on the dining table in my Brooklyn apartments over the years. They have been put through the test of being served to real live guests, some of them many times, and I promise you they work.

Yes, all the recipes in this book are gluten-free, because I have to eat gluten-free, but you can always add bread (regular or gluten-free), and the very few recipes that use all-purpose gluten-free flour can also be made with regular all-purpose flour. I firmly believe in accommodating any and all dietary restrictions when entertaining, so I've clearly marked my menus with what diets they accommodate, using the icons that follow:

gluten-free   vegan   meat-free   dairy-free   pescatarian

Each menu also includes suggestions for how to revise or add to the meal if needed to accommodate additional dietary restrictions. Dietary restrictions are here to stay, so it's good to know how to roll with the needs of your guests.

I hope this book will inspire and help you gather people around your table for dinner. It's time to have more dinner parties!

Why I Host

Before I dive into sharing my recipes and advice for hosting, I thought I should try to explain why. The day after a dinner party when the thank-you texts from friends start to roll in, I always respond with, "Thank YOU for coming!" And no, that's not to be cute. I truly feel so grateful for anyone who shows up at my table and trusts their night to me.

Hosting a dinner party makes me feel useful and accomplished, but it also brings me great pleasure and joy. We could talk about how, as an introverted extrovert and formerly shy person, having a task and a structure gives me permission to be social, and that does play a part for sure, but that's not really it. Have you ever acted in a play? I did a lot of theater in my school and college days, and I loved the thrill of sharing a live performance with an audience after spending a long time carefully rehearsing and building it with the cast and crew. After all that work was over, we moved on with our lives. You might think, "What was all that effort for, if the thing you created just lasted for a moment?" But the memory of that performance and how it brought us all together in a new and exciting way lived on and left a lingering glow. Hosting a dinner party is like that for me. I love the buildup. I love the anticipation. I love setting my table in the afternoon glow of an empty house knowing that soon that table will be full of people. Fork by fork, glass by glass, I build the scene for the evening's experience, full of hope. And the next day as I wash wine glasses, I love to remember the evening, recount its best parts, and bask in the glow of something good that can never be duplicated or experienced again.

Another thing I love about hosting is the simple act of feeding people. It delights me to be able to watch something I made bring joy to another person as they eat it—and to know that I'm literally helping them *live* by feeding them is a special kind of magic. What other kind of gift could be a clearer sign of my love than nourishment? I've spent more time than I'd like living alone as an adult, and cooking for myself is a completely different experience than cooking for others. I prefer the latter but am working on getting better at the former. Dinner especially is a meal best shared. It is a time to stop and reflect on the day, to share your thoughts and experiences, to give thanks, and to nourish more than just the body. So, I bring as many people as I can into my home as often as I can. And when you have company to feed, you also have company to help do the dishes. And yes, I always let my company help throughout the night, even with the dishes—I do not believe in doing absolutely everything for anyone. That is not what hosting is about. It's about setting the stage for a memorable night, cooking some food, and sharing your love.

A LITTLE DINNER PARTY
PLANNING ADVICE

Old-fashioned etiquette guides, party-planning timelines, and RSVPs make me weak in the knees. But don't worry, I'm not here to impose that kind of structure onto your dinner party planning—we live in the modern world and don't have the time or the need for so much etiquette. But I do have some tips to make the process of hosting fit more easily into your life.

THE MORE OFTEN YOU HOST,
THE EASIER IT BECOMES

I suppose this is true for most things in life, right? So, if you want to become good at hosting, make a habit of having people over. Put a dinner party on the calendar at least once a month! The more you do it, the easier it gets. And the easier it gets, the less you'll worry about it and the more you'll want to do it.

THERE IS NO PERFECT NUMBER OF GUESTS

How many people should you invite? Well, that's really up to you. Four people can feel like a party if that's not the usual number at your table. And many of the menus in this book can even be cut down to serve two. My table seats eight most comfortably, so that's usually the number I aim for myself, but often I get overexcited with invitations and end up with ten or twelve. Try to keep it under twelve though—more than that and it's hard to have meaningful conversation, let alone fit everyone around the table.

You can dive as deep into the puzzle of who to host together at your table as you want. Some people say that for the ideal dinner party guest list you should make sure that each person you invite knows at least one person other than you, and that there is at least one person each guest does not know. At this point I've hosted too many dinner parties already, and all my friends have now become friends with each other from being introduced at my table, so I'm running out of people in my life who don't know each other to be able to play the guest list game that way. But I do try to mix things up. Sometimes I invite only couples. Sometimes I invite only ladies. Sometimes I have no control over my list because it's Easter and I'm cooking for my extended family.

If I don't have a clear vision of whom my guest list should include, I build it piece by piece. I send a text to one friend who I've been meaning to have over to see if they're available on my chosen date, and then if they are, I invite the next guest who I think will fit well with them, and so on and so forth as each person I reach out to accepts or declines until my table is full. This method is much safer than sending out a group email where everyone else can see who's invited on the first go—that way no one knows who was in the first or second or third round of invites. Once everyone is confirmed, I send out a Google calendar invitation so they can see who else is coming and have the details of the event on their calendar. If paper invitations or Paperless Post are your thing, by all means, indulge in that process.

ALWAYS ASK ABOUT DIETARY RESTRICTIONS

As soon as a guest confirms your invite, ask (if you don't already know) if they have any dietary restrictions. Knowing this in advance helps you pick a menu that will suit all of your guests' needs. Do not question or judge anyone's dietary restrictions, please. Go with the flow and accommodate; it's just easier and more fun for everyone that way.

A TIMELINE IS HELPFUL

It is completely possible to decide to host a dinner party in the afternoon and pull it off by dinnertime. And some of the menus in this book are perfect for that (see page 59 or 205). I love a spontaneous dinner party. But I love a planned dinner party even more. I like to see it on my calendar for a couple weeks, winking at me and glittering with anticipation. Depending on how scheduled your life is, pick a date and time and invite guests anywhere between two months and two hours before dinner. For most, two weeks in advance is the perfect amount of notice. Once you have your date set, you can fit your prep in as leisurely or condensed of a timeline as your schedule allows. Whatever the case may be, take a moment and write down all the things that you need to do before your guests arrive. Then organize them by the time they need to be done by and tackle them in the appropriate order. In each of the menus in this book, I give you tips for managing the prep timeline.

Menu aside, here are my general timeline tips for low-stress dinner party prep, assuming you have at least a week to get ready.

One Week Before

- Invite and/or confirm guests for your dinner party. Don't forget to ask about dietary restrictions.

- Decide on your menu.

- Stock up on all the wine and booze needed for hosting.

Three to Four Days Before

- Clean the house, or at least the parts of the house your guests will see when they come for dinner.

- Procure all groceries needed for your menu.

Day Before

- Make dessert, if baking something.

- Prep as much food as you can/want to.

- Make place cards for the table and a seating chart if you're going to assign seats.

- Put fresh candles in candlesticks, if needed.

- Buy fresh flowers for the table if you want. I always like having fresh flowers around.

- Make fresh ice or purchase extra ice. There's nothing worse than realizing you're out of ice when you want to make a few cocktails— but making cocktails with stale old ice is a close second.

Morning Before

- Set the table. Having this done early gives me a great sense of calm. But if you'd rather not, or can't, it's a very good task to assign to the first couple guests who arrive.

- Prep as much food as you can.

One Hour Before Guests Arrive

- Clean the kitchen. Whatever cooking that's left to be done will need to be done with guests, and that's all OK. So, stop and clean now.

- Shower, dress, and reset yourself. You need to be ready too, not just your home and the food.

- Assemble snacks and drinks so they're available as soon as guests start arriving.

Ten Minutes Before Guests Arrive

- Dim the lights everywhere in the house, and make sure lights are on in all the rooms and bathrooms guests will be using. Light some candles here and there.

- Turn on some music.

ASSIGNED SEATING IS FUN SOMETIMES

If I'm hosting more than six people and at least two of them don't know everyone at the table, I will assign seating. If all my guests are old friends, I usually won't. But I love the practice of meditating over my guest list, penciling and erasing initials from around the table I draw in my notebook until I see a seating formation that will provide security and amusement for each of my guests and balance the dynamic of the table. This is my kind of puzzle solving. I also love making place cards for my guests and having them all set out on the table when people arrive. Finding a place card with your name on it at the table is exciting and can make the whole occasion feel a little bit more special.

IT'S NOT ALL ABOUT THE FOOD

Hosting a dinner party is only half about the food. Don't spend all your time paying attention to and assembling and administering food. Once your guests arrive, try to pay attention to them instead. The party will go better and will be more meaningful for your guests as well as for you if you are able to focus on hosting the party rather than cooking for the party once it starts. My menus are designed to help you do this, but it also helps to hold that intention in your mind. Even after years of hosting I can get lost in the food and have to pull myself out of it. Be present in the party. Be a good leader. It's your job to herd your herd: Make introductions, enable transitions between spaces and activities, help steer conversations, give a toast or two, and radiate the attitude you want to see into your party.

ASK FOR HELP

Cooking for people as well as hosting can be a lot of work. There is no shame in asking for help. When your guests arrive and you're behind schedule with your dinner prep (which, FYI, is actually still what happens to me every single time I host), put them to work! Offer them a drink first, and then assign a task. I promise they'll love feeling helpful and included. It's also OK to ask one of your friends to come early to help you get ready, or to hire a house cleaner to clean for you before a party, or to ask your partner or family for extra help, or to seek out any other kind of assistance you need. You do not need to single-handedly host a dinner party. And most importantly, you do not need to do all the dishes. If someone offers to do dishes, say yes! If no one offers, turn up the dance music and ask people to join you in a dish-washing party. Just leave the wine glasses for the next morning. You'll break them if you try to wash them at the end of a party, and your guests probably aren't done using them yet anyway.

NEVER APOLOGIZE

No matter how far behind schedule dinner gets, no matter if you burn the whole dinner and end up ordering pizza instead, no matter if your house is dirty, or you forgot to get extra toilet paper, or the cat keeps jumping on the table, or your baby keeps crying upstairs, or whatever may occur during your dinner party to distress you: Do not apologize. I promise that your guests are happy to be invited into your home for dinner, no matter if it meets your own personal expectations of how it should be or not. Laugh it off. Pour everyone another glass of wine. Play a game. Change the topic of conversation. Change the music. Do whatever you need to do to get the energy going the way you want it to go, but do not apologize or explain your failings. Doing so will actually point these things out to guests who would otherwise not have noticed, and it will make them feel sorry for you and like they need to soothe and help you rather than continue to enjoy your company and your party. (Don't let your guests apologize either if they spill wine on your white tablecloth or break your grandma's china, which will happen, and which is totally not worth getting upset about.)

THE DINNER PARTY–READY KITCHEN

I try not to ask for any too-specialized equipment or ingredients in any of my recipes, and if I do I promise it's because it's worth it, like a kitchen torch for making crème brûlée. Beyond the expected knives and pots and pans and measuring utensils needed for general cooking, here are some kitchen tools that will make the menus in this book, and hosting dinner parties in general, easier in your kitchen.

ONE 9-INCH (23-CM) CAKE PAN

All the cake recipes in this book are 9-inch (23-cm) cakes, and with the exception of one, they're all baked in a standard 9-inch (23-cm) cake pan. This doesn't need to be nonstick or anything fancy, but you certainly need one. And if you ever see a layer cake in your future, you might as well get two. I also highly recommend treating yourself to a package of 9-inch (23-cm) round parchment cake pan liners, which you can find at a cake supply shop or order online. They save time and fuss while baking and are incredibly satisfying to use.

ONE 9-INCH (23-CM) SPRINGFORM PAN

Yes, you need both types of cake pans. This one has higher sides and the ability to release the sides from the base, which is essential for delicate things like the Polenta-Crusted Deep-Dish Quiche (page 158) and Amaro-Chocolate Cloud Cake (page 249) in this book, or for a cheesecake. Worth having!

AN ELECTRIC MIXER

A stand mixer or a simple little electric handheld mixer makes getting egg whites to stiff peaks so much easier. Of course, you can always do it by hand, but if baking is a part of your entertaining life, it's worth it to have some help.

A FOOD PROCESSOR OR A BLENDER

Even if it's just a mini food processor or a handheld immersion blender, whipping up sauces is so much easier with a little appliance power. I call for both a food processor and a blender in the recipes in this book.

A VERY LARGE BOWL

You need a bigger bowl—like the biggest possible metal mixing bowl you can find. It'll make tossing salads for a crowd easier. It'll make seasoning a big batch of vegetables for roasting easier. It'll make whipping cream by hand easier. Once you get one you won't know how you ever lived without it.

HALF SHEET PANS

This is super important: You need professional quality half sheet pans in your life. I use them for everything. Measuring 18 by 13 inches (46 by 35.5 cm) in size and about 1 inch (2.5 cm) deep, they're called half sheet pans because they're half the size of a full sheet pan, which are far too large for home ovens but are used in restaurant kitchens. I call them simply sheet pans, though some people refer to them as rimmed baking sheets. Untreated aluminum, preferably Nordic Ware brand, is the way to go, and they will last you a lifetime. Flimsy cookie trays are not a substitute here, sorry. I have six sheet pans in my kitchen, but for your purposes at least three will be enough. You should also get at least one wire cooling rack that fits perfectly inside a sheet pan—they're often sold as a set—and you'll see it's infinitely useful.

A LARGE DUTCH OVEN

By large, I mean large. At least 7- (6.6 L) and up to 10-quart (9.5 L) capacity large. Braises and stews and beans for a crowd require it.

AN INSTANT-READ THERMOMETER

It's never a good idea to guess if your meat is perfectly cooked. I always use an instant-read thermometer to know for sure. I like a Thermapen, but any instant-read thermometer is better than none.

STAIN REMOVER AND PAPER TOWELS

Your guests are going to spill wine. They will spill red wine on your white lace tablecloth and you will not worry about it at all because you will be prepared. Arm yourself with a good stain remover (I swear by the cheekily named Château Spill), some paper towels, and a good attitude. I try not to use paper towels in my daily life, but they are the best tool for mopping up impromptu spills of any kind, so I always keep a stash of them on hand.

And here are some things to keep in your pantry at all times, in no particular order:

LEMONS AND LIMES

For sauces, salad dressings, cocktails, and more. Keep them in the fridge at all times.

CHEESE FOR SNACKS

I like to keep a few hunks of nice cheese in the fridge at all times, because you never know when you'll need to put out a cheese snack when dinner is taking too long to cook, or serve instead of dessert if you actually didn't have time to bake that cake after all.

OLIVES AND/OR PICKLES

Also for snacks. They keep for a long time, so just have them in your fridge always. And also, you know, for martinis.

CRACKERS

Cheese snacks are better with crackers. And in a pinch, crackers on their own make a fine snack to put out for guests. I always keep at least three boxes of my favorite crackers in the pantry just in case. Find a favorite and do the same. I like Mary's Gone Crackers.

POTATO CHIPS

Nothing becomes an entertaining snack so easily as a bag of potato chips. I keep one or two hidden at all times—they're great on their own, but I've got some ways to jazz them up on page 20.

HEAVY CREAM

Heavy cream, thanks to its high fat content, keeps for a very long time in the fridge. Most desserts are better with whipped cream, and when there's no dessert, whipped cream can itself be The Dessert. So, keep a pint in the fridge at all times and you'll always be ready. Unless you're dairy-free, in which case obviously skip this one.

LOTS OF OLIVE OIL

Every time I bring a group of friends to my family lake house for a weekend, I buy all the groceries we need in advance, and I always, always run out of olive oil. It's become a standing joke. My friends don't know how I can run out of a whole bottle in one weekend. Well, I love olive oil, and I use it generously in all my menus. And a weekend of entertaining ten guests will completely deplete a bottle. So now I've learned to always bring a backup, and to always stock a backup in my house too. If you're feeling fancy, buy a special (usually expensive), more flavorful olive oil for finishing, and a milder, cheaper olive oil for cooking with. I don't get into that—I just buy a lot of one olive oil that tastes good for drizzling and is cheap enough for cooking with, such as California Olive Ranch, and I use it generously.

SHERRY VINEGAR

I've got a thing for sherry vinegar. If I had to live with only one vinegar for the rest of my life, she would be the one. Tart enough to pack a punch, sweet enough to not sting, and deep enough to intrigue. You'll see a lot of her in my recipes.

HARISSA PASTE

I use this earthy-spicy Moroccan red pepper sauce in a few recipes in this book, and often in my weeknight cooking. Depending on where you live, it may be hard to find. It's easy enough to order online (I love the one made by New York Shuk), so stock up on it in advance. Unopened, a jar keeps in the cupboard for a couple years.

CANNED BEANS

I always keep a few cans of beans in my pantry; not only do they come in handy for weeknight dinners, but they're lifesavers when an unexpectedly vegan guest shows up and I've already cooked a pork roast to serve. With some olive oil, herbs, and garlic, canned beans can become a very fast, like-you-planned-it, substitution to serve that vegan guest. I love Bioitalia butter beans if you can find them—they're the best tasting (and best looking!) canned white beans I've ever met.

DIJON MUSTARD

Can't live without it, i.e., can't make salad dressing, aioli, or mustard-braised pork without it. Keep an extra in the pantry and an open one in the fridge and never look back.

HONEY

My go-to sweetener, and secret sauce hero. Buy local if you can, which is going to be more expensive, but honey lasts a long time and good local honey is not only better for the environment but can taste so much more complex.

SALT

But of course, you say. But wait, let's talk about salt! You should always have two kinds in your kitchen: kosher salt for cooking with, and flaky sea salt for finishing. I use Diamond Crystal kosher salt, and that's what all the recipes in this book were developed and tested with. To ensure that your recipes are seasoned the same as mine, buy the same. For flaky, I like Maldon.

CHILE FLAKES

I like to have at least two kinds of chile flakes in my pantry at all times: one spicy and one milder. For a classic hit of hot pepper spice, I always have crushed red pepper flakes available. For milder, earthier spice, Aleppo-style pepper flakes are my go-to, but I also like to have slightly spicier and smokier Urfa biber chile flakes on hand as well.

CHOCOLATE

High up in the back of the top shelf of a pantry cupboard, I keep a stash of some really nice bars of dark chocolate to pull out for dessert (or second dessert) for guests when needed. I hide them this way because otherwise I would eat them all myself, but you do whatever works for you. Every host needs to have chocolate available, trust me, and see page 225 for some ideas on how to serve it.

WINE

When I host a dinner party, people always ask what they can bring. I like to control the whole menu (it's also just easier that way), so I always answer, "Bring some wine if you want!" But please do not count on your guests to bring *enough* wine. Inevitably one couple will arrive with one bottle of wine in hand then proceed to drink two bottles' worth of wine between the two of them. This is all OK and part of the fun; you just need to be prepared for it as the host. Having wine bottles in the house is not an unhealthy temptation or trigger for me, so I believe in having at least six bottles in my house at all times, and I always buy wine by the case from my favorite local wine store so I get a good discount on it. Find a local wine store you can get to know, and ask for their help picking wines within your budget—they're there to help you, don't be afraid to ask! When it comes time for a dinner party, I make sure I have as many bottles as drinking guests in my house for the night. And if all the guests show up with wine that matches the menu in enough quantity to last the night and my bottles don't get touched, that's fine too, because unopened wine does not go bad, and it'll be there for next time.

SELTZER

You should always have something to offer alcohol-free guests, and a nice flavored seltzer like Spindrift is a good option. For the table, a few big glass bottles of sparkling mineral water are what I serve at dinnertime. I buy S.Pellegrino by the case. If you're not a bubbly fan, put a pitcher or two of water on the table. Just make sure you're feeding your guests water along with wine.

For the end of the night, I like to keep a case of individual cans of seltzer chilling by my door. As guests leave, I give them each a can of seltzer for the road. When I lived in Brooklyn and everyone took Ubers home in the wee hours, this was especially appreciated. If the guests are staying the night, I just start handing out cans as people lounge in the living room. Hydration is important when seriously dinner partying.

Because hosting dinner also means setting the table, here are some things to make sure you have in your house to be able to set the table for guests. Of course not all these things need to be acquired in order to host a dinner party, they're merely suggestions for things to accumulate over time as you expand your hosting life.

CLOTH NAPKINS

I use cloth napkins for every meal. They're better for the environment than paper, they work better, and they look better. I love linen napkins best of all, which get softer as they age with every wash and dry. I think I have at least four dozen of them tucked into my credenza. You don't need to have that many, and they don't even need to all match, but you should have at least one dozen to be able to set a full table with cloth napkins for dinner.

CANDLES

A dinner party without candles is not a dinner party. Dim the lights, light candles on the table, and suddenly it doesn't matter what the rest of your home looks like because your table is an insulated, glowing, enticing world of its own. I like to use beeswax candles because they supposedly help purify rather than pollute the air inside your home, and they just smell and look so good. Place tapers in candle holders so that the flame is higher than the eyes of the person sitting across the table from you for ideal lighting and start the night with fresh tapers so you don't have to worry about changing candles.

PLATES

You should aim to have at least twelve dinner plates in the house. They don't have to match, and they don't have to be fancy or expensive, they just need to hold food. Thrift stores and flea markets are some of the best places to find cheap beautiful plates.

A FEW BIG PLATTERS

The name of the game here is platters, so you're going to need a few big platters for serving these menus. Or at least two. Again, hit your local thrift stores and flea markets or antique stores for some affordable good-looking platters, or search Etsy or eBay. I have a platter-collecting problem. Almost all the platters you see photographed in this book are ones I actually own that I've picked up all over the place over the years. They live in precariously tall stacks in my credenza, and I really do need to give some away, but I love them all so much.

ENOUGH GLASSES

You should have enough glasses for each guest to have one wine glass and one water glass. Which means at least a dozen wine glasses and at least a dozen water glasses. Again, they don't need to match, you just need to have them. If you think you'll never host more than eight people, then have at least eight of each. Wine glasses don't have to be actual wine glasses, they can be any glass. Just have enough glasses for every guest to use two at once.

CUTLERY

I'm starting to repeat myself here, so you already know what I'm going to say. You need at least a dozen place settings. They don't need to match. It's nice to have a set of steak knives to put out when sliceable meat is being served.

SOME SERVING UTENSILS

A large spoon or two and a serving fork or two are really all you need for serving utensils. You can find lovely and affordable ones at almost any flea market or antique store. A pair of serving tongs is nice to have too and/or a set of salad servers.

AN ICE BUCKET

This is totally *not* essential, but once you have one, you'll realize how useful it really is. If you spend any time browsing flea markets, consignment shops, or Etsy you will stumble across an ice bucket. If it catches your eye, buy it. Fill it with ice for a spritz station before dinner. Fill it with ice and plop it next to a few bottles for after-dinner drinks. It keeps the ice cold longer, it makes the ice easier to reach, and it just looks cute and sets the mood. I own three, which is probably too many, but how could I resist? (And I use them!) A pair of ice tongs (if one didn't come with the bucket, which sometimes they do) is a helpful thing to have too.

Hello! Come in! Welcome! Can I get you a drink? This moment sets the tone for the rest of the night. It says: This is a party, not just dinner. It says: You are my guest, I care about you, and I'm going to take care of you. It eases the transition from whatever outside world they're coming from into the world of your home. It's a simple gesture, but a meaningful ritual of welcome. I always offer two choices: seltzer as the first and then, depending on my mood, the weather, and the occasion, either a spritz, a martini, or a glass of wine. I like to serve spritzes if it's hot, but also if I want something lighter in alcohol to ease into the evening more slowly. I set up a spritz station so guests can DIY their drink, or so I can easily assemble each as people arrive. Martinis are for getting the party started more quickly, or for Friday nights, or chilly nights. Wine is for weeknights, for larger crowds, or for when I don't have time to assemble even the simplest of cocktails.

To make a **spritz station**, you need: a bottle of aperitif bitters such as Campari, Cappelletti, Contratto, or Forthave Spirits Red; a bottle (or two) of sparkling wine; a bottle (or two) of sparkling water; a bucket of ice; and a bowl of garnish—either sliced oranges or olives or both. For each serving, fill a glass with ice, pour in a shot of aperitif bitters, fill the glass halfway with sparkling wine, then finish filling with sparkling water and garnish as desired. Give each cocktail a stir before serving or serve with cocktail stirrers for guests to stir their own. (The red liquor will stay on the bottom of the glass until stirred.)

To make **martinis** for a dinner party, I always make a pitcher of 50/50 martinis—half vermouth and half gin. Calculate 2 ounces of gin and 2 ounces of dry vermouth per guest, then pour it all into an appropriately sized pitcher. So, if you'll be six people for dinner, you'll want 12 ounces (360 ml) of each, or 1½ cups of each. Just before guests arrive, add as much ice as will fit in the pitcher, and stir it well with a cocktail stirrer or long spoon. To serve, simply pour out a small glass at a time and garnish with an olive or a lemon twist or both. The martini mixture in the pitcher will dilute as it sits, but I really don't think that's a bad thing.

If it's a **wine-to-start** night, I like to serve something bubbly or slightly fizzy and light and preferably cold. Talk to your favorite local wine shop about what you're looking for; they'll help you find the perfect bottle. A few current favorites of mine are:

Poggio delle Baccanti—"Gragnano" Rosso Frizzante: a very fizzy, very juicy sparkling Italian red, best served cold with cheese snacks. For a similar fun-filled fizz, look for any chilled red Lambrusco.

Hervé Rafflin—"La Nature'l" Extra Brut Champagne NV: an organic, crowd-pleasing, dry, affordable, fill-your-nose-with-bubbles grower Champagne for any occasion. For the best flavor for your money when it comes to Champagne, look for a "grower champagne" at your local store, which means it's made and bottled by the same person growing the grapes.

Meinklang—"Prosa" Burgenland Sparkling Rosé: pretty and frothy in pink, but dry, clever, and very easy to drink. Buy extra. If you can't find it, ask your wine shop for their favorite pét-nat instead.

THERE SHOULD ALWAYS BE SNACKS

When you're hosting a dinner party, you absolutely do not need to serve appetizers or a first course or fussy small-bite things. If that's what you want to do, host a cocktail party instead. The focus here is dinner, so focus on dinner, and put out a little something yummy to nibble while you and your guests drink and chat beforehand. One or two snacks is enough. These are my favorite no- to low-cook snacks to put out at any time of day, but especially when guests arrive before dinner. I've constructed these recipes so you can easily scale them up or down to suit the size of your pantry.

A FANCY EGG SNACK

Large eggs, 1 per person

Aioli (page 41) or olive oil

Flaky salt

Something to sprinkle on top, such as mild chile flakes, chopped herbs, or furikake

Deviled eggs are fun, but a lot of work to make. Instead, I make A Fancy Egg Snack, which just means jammy eggs topped with fun things to feel fancy. By *jammy* I mean the yolk, which I cook to a jam-like consistency halfway between soft boiled and hard boiled.

Up to two days before serving, boil and peel the eggs. Bring a large pot of water to a boil, then using a spoon, gently lower however many eggs you're cooking into the water and cook for 7 minutes. Drain, then cover the eggs in ice water until cool enough to touch. While they cool, tap the tops of each egg against the side of the pot just until it cracks a bit, which breaks the seal of the albumen and lets some water in under the shell to make the egg easier to peel. Peel all the eggs, dry them, and then stash them in a container in the fridge until ready to serve.

Slice each egg lengthwise in half and arrange on a serving platter. Top each with a dollop of aioli or a drizzle of olive oil, then sprinkle flaky salt and something else all over the top.

DOLLED-UP POTATO CHIPS

Potato chips are the perfect drinking snack. Salty, crunchy, crispy, festive—no one will ever be mad to see a potato chip. Before I tell you how to doll up potato chips, I have to tell you that most of the time I actually just put out a bowl of plain potato chips. Putting them in a fancy bowl (or in a bowl at all, rather than eating out of the bag) dolls them up already. After growing up in New England, I'm devoted to Cape Cod original potato chips, but you can choose your favorite full-fat, full-salt classic potato chip, then put it on a pedestal and serve it with pride. If you want to fuss with the flavor and doll them up further, sprinkle some lemon zest and mild chile flakes on top. Or add some freshly ground black pepper and a sprinkle of finely chopped dill. Any spice and herb or citrus zest will happily land on a potato chip and elevate them to fancy homemade snack status.

THERE SHOULD ALWAYS BE SNACKS

You know what goes great next to a fancy bowl full of potato chips at cocktail hour? A plate of cold, fresh fruit. If they're in season, make that fruit cherries. To make the cherries extra cold, add ice cubes to the platter. Seriously, if you have never tried the combination of cherries and potato chips, please do. It tastes like the first day of summer vacation, and pairs quite well with a G&T. Later in the summer, make it a platter of cold melon slices doused in lime juice and sprinkled with Tajín (or just flaky salt). If it's winter, swap in orange wedges sprinkled with Tajín or flaky salt. In the fall, fresh figs, simply torn into halves, require no topping.

FRUIT SNACKS

THE GO-TO CUCUMBER AND RADISH SNACK

Mini (Persian) seedless cucumbers,
   1 per person
Daikon radish, 1 or 2 big ones, and
   maybe a watermelon radish too
   for some fun color. (If you can't
   find either, just use standard pink
   radishes, about 2 per person.)
Some acid, such as rice vinegar or
   lemon juice
Flaky sea salt
Mild chile flakes for sprinkling, such
   as Aleppo-style or Urfa biber

I love mini cucumbers so much. They're basically just crunchy water, but add some acid and some salt and all the sudden they're so much more. It's like snacking on bar snacks that are somehow also refreshing and light. I like to pair them with rounds of spicy white daikon radishes, which makes these cucumbers seem sweet by comparison. I'd say about seventy-five percent of my dinner parties start with a plate of this snack and some potato chips, and I'm still not sick of it.

Wash and slice the cucumbers into spears. Peel the daikon and slice it into rounds. Ditto if you're using watermelon radish. If you've got small regular pink radishes, slice them into halves or quarters depending on their size. Toss the lot in a bit of your acid of choice (I like unseasoned rice vinegar best for this) and let it sit for a few minutes, up to 30 minutes. Sprinkle with salt and chile flakes before serving. Repeat often.

THE STEAMED ARTICHOKE TRICK

1 artichoke for every 2 guests

1 lemon, halved

Aioli (page 41) or melted
    salted butter, about ¼ cup
    per artichoke, for dipping

I call it a trick because I do have a helpful technique for it, but also because serving this as your welcome snack is a great way to trick your guests into having a good time right away. Eating a whole artichoke from the outer leaves all the way to the sweet heart is one of the most fun things. Tear, dip, and scrape the flesh off the base of each leaf with your teeth, then discard. It's a snack that keeps your hands busy. It's not formal or glamorous, but there's something kind of sexy about the act. Make it a whole platter of steamed artichoke halves with the choke already cleaned out for easier eating, and it's an unexpected hands-on ice-breaker for your guests. This is a moment for serving tart, cold white wine, perhaps a Grüner Veltliner, which the artichoke will make taste sweeter.

You can prep and steam your artichokes anytime between 1 day and 1 hour before serving. Fill a large pot fitted with a steamer insert with a few inches of water and heat to a boil. Meanwhile, prep the artichokes: Slice the pointed top (about 1 inch of it) off each artichoke and discard, then trim just the very end of the stem and slice the artichoke in half down through the stem. Rub lemon all over the sliced interiors. Using a small spoon, scoop out and discard the hairy choke, leaving as many leaves around it as possible. Rub that lemon all over the scraped heart. Repeat with all your artichokes, then pile them in the steamer insert, squeeze any remaining lemon juice over the top, cover with a lid, and steam until the artichokes can be easily pierced with a fork, about 20 minutes. Let cool to room temperature. If not serving within a couple hours, pack them up and chill them until ready to serve with a small bowl of aioli or melted butter for dipping.

A MEAT AND PICKLES SNACK

I love cured meats in all forms, but they can be a lot of salt and fat without some pickles to balance them out. One of my favorite cocktail snacks is simply that: a plate of pickles and cured meats. It goes especially well with a spritz, the sweet-bitter fizz balancing it out just right. This snack can be as simple as salami and cornichons, or as complex as a grand spread of sliced prosciutto, salami, coppa, and bresaola with pickled carrots, cornichons, dilly beans, and pickled beets. If you have a place to buy fresh thinly sliced cured meats, that's always best, but if you don't, the packaged pre-sliced kind is fine. Try to look for a nitrate-free option. To make round slices of cured meat more appealing and easier to pick up, I fold them in quarters then arrange on the platter, where they sort of puff up like little meat flowers. This one's not for vegetarian guests, but great for the dairy free.

CHEESE SNACKS
MY WAY

If serving cheese for more than two or three people, I do not like to serve a selection of cheeses. I know this is controversial, but hear me out. I love a good cheese board to share with a date. In fact, this is a favorite dinner substitute. But when there's a crowd, that cheese board becomes mangled so fast. The blue cheese knife gets dunked in the triple cream, or someone hogs all the Manchego. There are cheese crumbs on the floor. It's not a thing for a crowd, even a small crowd. Instead, I pick one big piece of cheese and stick to it. One cheese on its own plate with one knife and then there's less mess, less contamination, less inequality, and no one fills up on too much cheese before dinner.

Sticking with one cheese doesn't mean you can't have a spread of things to go with it though. I add a bowl of crackers; some kind of fruit such as sliced apples, pears, figs, fresh grapes, dried figs, or apricots; and then something salty and briny like olives or pickles. If I'm feeling extra, I'll add something for drizzling too, like honey or jam, but that can get messy with a crowd, so tread carefully.

SKILLET SOCCA TO SERVE WITH ANY SAUCE

1 cup (118 g) chickpea
(garbanzo bean) flour
4 tablespoons (60 ml) olive
oil, divided
1 teaspoon kosher salt
Flaky sea salt, for topping
Any sauce, for serving

SERVES 4 TO 6

The Provençal flatbread known as socca is crispy, deeply savory, and naturally gluten-free—reason enough to always keep chickpea flour in your pantry. (Then you can keep using it for traditional Indian cooking and gluten-free baking, too.) I like to serve socca as an appetizer with a sauce or two, but also on the table as a gluten-free bread substitute. Socca plays well with almost any of the sauces in this book, but I especially love it with Blender Spiced Green Sauce (page 43).

Place a rack in the top third of your oven and preheat to 450°F (230°C). In a medium bowl or large measuring cup, whisk the chickpea flour, 2 tablespoons of the oil, the salt, and 1 cup (240 ml) of water until combined. Let sit at least 10 minutes and up to 1 hour to allow the flour to hydrate.

Heat the remaining 2 tablespoons of the oil in a 12-inch (30.5-cm) cast-iron skillet over high until shimmering. Pour in the chickpea batter and tilt to evenly coat the skillet. Transfer to the oven and bake the flatbread until the top is golden brown and crisped, 20 to 25 minutes. Carefully invert the skillet over a large cutting board. Slice into wedges and transfer to a serving platter. Sprinkle with flaky salt and serve with any sauce for dipping.

SAUCES AND TOPPINGS FOR ALL SEASONS

Dinner is more fun with some kind of homemade sauce or topping on the table. Make that two sauces or topping options and it's a double-the-fun, choose-your-own-topping adventure. The recipes in my book are simple, and while they're still delicious on their own, serving them together as a menu with a sauce is what turns them into something truly occasion-worthy. The sauces that follow are all used in at least a few menus throughout the book; some menus use two, and very few use none. And, of course, you can mix and match them as you wish. These sauces are good for more than your dinner parties though. They will jazz up simple cooking any night of the week. Serve liberally and often.

GARLICKY YOGURT SAUCE

2 cups (480 ml) plain full-fat
    Greek yogurt
2 tablespoons lemon juice
1 large or 2 small cloves
    garlic, finely grated
1 teaspoon kosher salt

MAKES ABOUT 2 CUPS
(480 ML)

Anytime you're serving something spicy, yogurt sauce is here to calm everyone down. It's also here to add moisture and richness to anything feeling a little bit dry or bland. It's the cold creamy counterpoint to so many meals at my table. I like it with lots of raw garlic (and yes, one clove is lots of garlic in yogurt sauce), so feel free to use less or omit the garlic entirely if you're not up for it.

In a medium bowl, whisk together the yogurt, lemon juice, garlic, and salt until smooth. If you want your sauce a little runnier, add a bit of cold water, 1 teaspoon at a time, until it's the right consistency. The sauce keeps chilled in a sealed container for up to 5 days.

PICKLED SHALLOT SALSA VERDE

2 shallots, finely chopped

¼ cup (60 ml) sherry or red wine vinegar

1 teaspoon kosher salt

¼ cup (7 g) fresh oregano leaves, finely chopped

1 cup (30 g) fresh parsley leaves and tender stems, finely chopped

1 cup (30 g) fresh basil or mint leaves, finely chopped

1 cup (240 ml) olive oil

MAKES ABOUT 1½ CUPS (360 ML)

Of all the sauces in this book, this is the one I serve most often at my table. It's got everything I want in a sauce: pickley zesty tang, herbal freshness, richness, and texture. It brightens up everything it touches. Though it may be tempting to process all those herbs in the food processor, it's best to chop the herbs and make the sauce by hand to keep the distinct texture and freshness of the herbs.

In a small bowl, stir the shallots, vinegar, and salt together and let sit at room temperature to pickle for at least 15 minutes and up to 3 hours.

In a separate small bowl, stir together the finely chopped herbs and olive oil. You can do this up to 3 hours before serving as well; let sit at room temperature.

Just before serving, combine the shallot mixture and herb mixture. Taste and add more salt if needed. You want to keep the shallots and the herbs separate until the last minute because as soon as the acid is introduced to the herbs, it will slowly start to break down and brown them, and that's just not pretty or fresh tasting.

CRISPY GARLIC AND CHILI OIL

1 cup (240 ml) neutral
    oil, such as sunflower,
    safflower, or grapeseed
10 cloves garlic, thinly sliced
2 tablespoons crushed red
    pepper flakes
1 teaspoon tamari
1 teaspoon honey

MAKES ABOUT 1 CUP
(240 ML)

Spicy, crunchy, and completely addictive, this chili oil is in my fridge at all times. It livens up everything it touches and is not too spicy for the spice-averse. A mandoline comes in handy here for thinly slicing all the garlic, but you can also do it by hand.

In a small pot, heat the oil and garlic over medium heat. Cook, swirling occasionally, until the garlic is golden-brown and crisp. Pour into a medium mixing bowl and stir in the pepper flakes, tamari, and honey. Let cool to room temperature then chill in an airtight container for up to 2 weeks.

CHARRED SCALLION
SPOON SAUCE

1 bunch green onions

1 tablespoon neutral oil, such
    as sunflower, safflower, or
    grapeseed

½ cup (120 ml) olive oil

1 cup (155 g) pitted
    green olives, such as
    Castelvetrano, crushed

Zest of 1 lemon, finely grated

1 tablespoon Aleppo-style
    pepper flakes

½ teaspoon kosher salt

MAKES ABOUT 1 CUP
(240 ML)

Anytime you're firing up the grill, throw a bunch of green onions on first until soft and charred and smoky, and chop them up. Mix them with olives, chile flakes, and lemon zest in lots of your best olive oil and spoon the sauce over anything you grill for dinner, especially milder things like fish, chicken, and zucchini. But don't let the lack of a grill stop you from making this sauce; the green onions can just as easily be charred in a skillet.

Prepare a grill for high heat grilling or heat a large cast-iron skillet over high heat on the stove. Toss the green onions in the neutral oil and then sear, turning often, until lightly charred on all sides and softened, 6 to 8 minutes. Set aside until cool enough to touch, then coarsely chop, trimming and discarding root ends. Transfer to a small bowl and stir in the olive oil, olives, lemon zest, chile flakes, and salt. Let sit at room temperature for up to 3 hours before serving or chill in an airtight container for up to 2 days before serving. If chilled, remember to let sit at room temperature for about 1 hour before serving since the oil will solidify when cold.

CREAMY JALAPEÑO SAUCE

4 large or 6 small jalapeños

½ cup (120 ml) fresh lime
    juice

1 clove garlic

2 whole bunches fresh
    cilantro

1 cup (240 ml) neutral
    oil, such as sunflower,
    safflower, or grapeseed

Kosher salt

MAKES ABOUT 1½ CUPS
(360 ML)

Despite the name and texture, there's no dairy in this sauce. I fell in love with this Tex-Mex condiment because of Texas native and former coworker Rhoda Boone, who taught me that the creaminess comes from a magic emulsification of oil, herbs, and lime juice that happens in the blender. It's exactly what you want drizzled over any taco, or to liven up some simple grilled fish or chicken. It's also good on your eggs in the morning or stirred into rice.

Cut a small piece of flesh from each of your jalapeños and taste them. If any of them are too spicy, remove the seeds by cutting the jalapeños in half lengthwise and slicing the ribs and seeds out with a paring knife. Be careful not to touch the seeds with your hands. If the flesh isn't spicy, go ahead and cut the jalapeño in half and toss it, seeds and all, into the jar of a blender.

Add the lime juice and garlic to the jalapeños in the blender and puree until slightly chunky but broken down. Trim just the thickest stems from the base of each bunch of cilantro, then add to the blender along with the oil. Puree until a smooth sauce forms, stopping and scraping down the sides as needed. Season to taste with salt. This sauce is best served within a few hours of being made (you can keep it covered at room temperature until serving). Refrigerate leftovers in an airtight container.

AIOLI

2 small cloves garlic

2 large egg yolks

1 tablespoon (or more) lemon juice

½ teaspoon Dijon mustard

Kosher salt

½ cup (120 ml) neutral oil, such as sunflower, safflower, or grapeseed

½ cup (120 ml) olive oil

MAKES ABOUT 1 CUP (240 ML)

You can make this garlicky mayonnaise in a food processor or by hand. If you're nervous about achieving emulsification, the food processor is your best friend. If making by hand, grab a friend to help pour oil while you mix. It's a good party trick to make aioli by hand in front of people once you've got the hang of it. How eggs and oil transform into mayonnaise is one of the most magical bits of kitchen alchemy you can perform with a bowl and a whisk. Aioli (which, yes, despite its creamy nature is totally dairy-free) is good on just about everything from sandwiches to lamb to green beans, and honestly you could serve it with every single meal in this book and no one would mind.

TO MAKE IN A FOOD PROCESSOR

Pulse the garlic until finely chopped. Add the egg yolks, lemon juice, mustard, and a pinch of salt and pulse to combine. With the motor running, very slowly pour in about half of your neutral oil. Scrape down the sides of the food processor bowl with a rubber spatula, then continue to add oil with the motor running. Add olive oil in the same manner. Taste the sauce; if it's too thick, pulse in water 1 tablespoon at a time. Add more salt and/or lemon juice if needed.

TO MAKE BY HAND

Into a large mixing bowl, use a Microplane to finely grate the garlic. Add the egg yolks, lemon juice, mustard, and a pinch of salt and whisk to combine. Add about a tablespoon of neutral oil and whisk well to combine. You should start to see an emulsion forming at this point, meaning that the mixture is combining and thickening. Now slowly stream in the rest of the neutral oil, whisking constantly. It helps to have someone pour oil while you whisk, or you can rest your bowl on a nest of a dish towel so you can whisk with one hand and pour with the other without needing to hold the bowl. Add the olive oil in the same manner, whisking vigorously until fully incorporated. Taste and adjust seasoning as needed.

Aioli can be chilled in an airtight container for up to 4 days.

TAHINI SAUCE

½ cup (120 ml) tahini

2 tablespoons lemon juice

1 teaspoon kosher salt

MAKES ABOUT 1 CUP
(240 ML)

Middle Eastern tahini sauce is smooth and tasting of toasted sesame seeds with a hint of lemon. Tahini sauce is perfect anytime you want a decadently creamy, dairy-free sauce to add to anything that needs an extra dose of richness, like simple roasted vegetables or a crunchy raw salad.

In a small bowl, whisk together the tahini, lemon juice, salt, and ¼ cup of water until smooth. If the sauce is too thick, whisk in more water until a pourable consistency is reached.

The sauce can be stored in an airtight container in the fridge for up to 1 week. It will solidify when chilled, so either bring it to room temperature before serving or whisk in a small splash of warm water to loosen it.

BLENDER SPICED GREEN SAUCE

1 serrano chile, stemmed and
   cut into a few pieces

1 bunch fresh parsley,
   toughest stems trimmed

1 bunch fresh cilantro

1 clove garlic

1 teaspoon coriander seeds

1 teaspoon cumin seeds

1 cup (240 ml) olive oil

2 tablespoons apple cider
   vinegar

2 teaspoons kosher salt

MAKES ABOUT 1½ CUPS
(360 ML)

Inspired by the spicy North African herb sauce chermoula, this sauce is equal parts spicy, zesty, warming, and refreshing. It plays well against fatty meats and earthy roasted vegetables, and it stays fresh in the fridge longer than other green sauces.

In the jar of a blender or food processor, combine all of the ingredients and puree until smooth. That's it, really. This sauce keeps in an airtight container in the fridge for up to 4 days—just be sure to bring it to room temperature before serving, since the oil will make the sauce solidify when cold.

PICKLED ONIONS

1 cup (240 ml) apple cider
  vinegar

1 tablespoon kosher salt

1 tablespoon coriander seeds

1 teaspoon white sugar

2 cinnamon sticks

2 medium onions, thinly
  sliced

MAKES ABOUT 2 CUPS
(480 ML)

Sweet, tart, a little bit crunchy—there's hardly anything that doesn't taste better with pickled onions on top. Keep a jar of them in the fridge and start adding them to everything from salad to eggs to roasted vegetables.

In a medium pot, bring the vinegar, ½ cup (120 ml) water, salt, coriander, sugar, and cinnamon sticks to a boil over high heat. Remove from the heat, add the onions, stir to combine, and let cool to room temperature in pot. Once cool, transfer to a resealable container and stash in the fridge for about 5 days.

GREMOLATA

1 cup (30 g) parsley leaves, finely chopped

½ cup (70 g) roasted nuts or seeds such as almonds, pistachios, hazelnuts, or sunflower seeds, finely chopped

Zest of 1 lemon, finely grated

1 garlic clove, finely grated

2 teaspoons flaky sea salt

MAKES ABOUT 1 CUP
(240 ML)

Sprinkle this Italian topping over anything you want to add some crunch and zing to. You can use any kind of nut (or seed if you're accommodating a nut allergy!), depending on personal preferences or what you have on hand. It will taste too strong on its own, but once sprinkled over braised meats, a bowl of creamy pasta, a salad, or roasted vegetables, it will be perfect, I promise. Just don't sprinkle it in addition to salt—this should be used in place of salt.

In a small bowl, toss together all of the ingredients right before serving.

LEMONY VINAIGRETTE

2 tablespoons lemon juice

2 tablespoons olive oil

½ teaspoon Dijon mustard

¼ teaspoon honey

¼ teaspoon kosher salt

MAKES ABOUT ¼ CUP
(60 ML), ENOUGH TO
DRESS A SALAD FOR 6

My go-to light and bright salad dressing. Use this to dress any lettuce for a simple green salad to serve with any meal. To reduce the number of dishes in my life, I usually make salad dressing right in my salad bowl.

In a small bowl (or salad bowl, if dressing salad to serve), whisk together the lemon juice, olive oil, mustard, honey, and salt until well combined. Taste and adjust seasoning if needed. Chill in an airtight container for up to 1 week; re-whisk before serving.

50

FOR THE TABLE

PICKLED PEPPERCORN VINAIGRETTE

2 tablespoons apple cider
vinegar

3 tablespoons olive oil

1 teaspoon honey

½ teaspoon kosher salt

1 tablespoon pickled green
peppercorns or capers,
drained and finely
chopped

1 tablespoon whole-grain
(old-style) mustard

MAKES ABOUT ⅓ CUP
(75 ML), ENOUGH TO DRESS
A SALAD FOR 6 OR DRIZZLE
OVER MEAT FOR 4

When you want a salad dressing with some fun pops of texture and flavor, try this one. It's also great drizzled over slow-cooked meats or roasted vegetables to brighten things up.

In a small bowl, whisk together the vinegar, olive oil, honey, and salt until combined, then whisk in the peppercorns and mustard. Taste, and adjust seasoning if needed. Chill in an airtight container for up to 1 week; re-whisk before serving.

THE RIGHT WAY TO MAKE A SALAD

You'll see in many of the menus that follow I have a Simple Salad as an optional add-on. I love a simple salad with most every dinner. It adds brightness and freshness and a healthy dose of green things. But I'm very particular about how to prep that salad. It might sound overly fussy but please try it my way; I think you'll see a difference and want to eat more salads. Here's how.

PICK THE RIGHT GREENS.

Please don't buy that box of spring mix from the grocery store. Chances are half of it is already wilted inside, and if not, it'll wilt and get slimy so fast once you bring it home. Choose a box of baby arugula instead—it will stay fresh longer, and it's always so refreshing. My other favorite simple salad green, which can be a bit harder to find, is little gem lettuce. It's so cute and crunchy and sweet. For even more crunch, go with romaine hearts. For more tenderness, pick a head or two of Boston, Bibb, or other butter lettuce. For more earthiness, select a head of whatever local leaf lettuce looks good to you.

Whatever you choose, discard any wilted or browned or bruised leaves. Trim the base and separate the leaves. If the leaves are big, tear them very gently into bite-size pieces.

WASH THE GREENS WELL.

A salad spinner is the best way to wash salad greens, but if you don't have one, fill a large bowl with cold water, swish your leaves around in there with your hands, then lift the leaves out of the bowl, shake, and transfer to clean dish towels. You want to lift them out of the water like this so that any dirt and sand stays on the bottom of the bowl of water and not on your lettuce.

AIR-DRY THE GREENS IN ADVANCE.

Even if you've washed and spin-dried your leaves in a salad spinner, they will still have some water on them, which will make them wilt faster and cause any dressing you try to toss them in to run off the leaves like so many tears. So, after you've washed your greens, lay them out in a single layer on a clean dish towel and place them in a cool place (not in direct sunlight or on your stovetop with the oven on please) until they are truly dry. Don't let them sit out too long, or they will start to wilt. Handwashed but not spun-dry lettuce will take longer to air-dry and should probably be transferred from one towel to another dry one halfway through drying to speed the process.

STORE THE GREENS VERY CAREFULLY.

Once the lettuce is dry, wrap it up in a loose bundle inside the damp dish towel it's on and transfer it to your salad bowl, then tuck it in the fridge or another cool place until ready to serve your salad. If your bowl won't fit, very carefully tuck the bundle into a plastic bag and hide it in the fridge for up to six hours.

DRESS THE SALAD WITH YOUR HANDS.

Do not try to dress a salad before serving—it will wilt. I like my simple salad dressed with Lemony Vinaigrette (page 48) most days, or Pickled Peppercorn Vinaigrette (page 51) when I want something a little more assertive. Pour your salad dressing down the side of the bowl and then use your hands to very gently lift and toss the salad leaves until they're coated in dressing. That's it. Don't get any tongs involved except for serving; they'll just damage the lettuce you worked so hard to get ready to eat.

FALL

FALL MENUS

I have never escaped my schoolgirl attachment to the year starting fresh in the fall. Fall is my favorite. It is the abundant harvest season, the time when it finally cools enough to turn on the oven, and when everyone's back in town from their summer vacations and ready to come over for dinner. Fall is also always a return to more involved cooking for me, a return to indoor dinners, to table linens and more candles, and to hosting more often. The menus that follow are arranged in order from early fall to late fall, but really, they all work anytime during the season, and some during the winter as well.

A SPICY TOMATOEY FISH AND CHARRED BROCCOLINI SALAD DINNER

Tiny orange sungold tomatoes stay sweet all the way to the end of tomato season. I love the way their tart sweetness pairs with spicy, smoky harissa paste, and this menu is all about that happy marriage. It's also all about getting the most out of the end of tomato season by roasting sungolds into a sauce for the fish.

Party Size	Sauce to Serve (choose one!)	Special Diets
Serves 8, easily halved to serve 4	Aioli (page 41)	
	Garlicky Yogurt Sauce (page 32)	
Party Prep		
The full menu can be cooked right before serving, in less than an hour.	**Optional Add-Ons**	
	Bread for mopping	

PLANNING ADVICE

- This menu is best cooked right before serving, and it doesn't take long to come together, so you could cook it all just ahead of dinnertime. But if you have the time, prep some in advance.

  - Prep the fish and chill in the fridge up to 6 hours in advance if desired.

  - Prep the tomatoes in harissa and let sit at room temperature up to 2 hours in advance.

  - Prep the broccolini and radicchio and have it all tossed in oil on a sheet pan before your guests arrive, that way you can slide it in the oven as soon as you pull the fish and tomatoes out.

- Don't worry about serving the fish piping hot—if it's done before you're ready to sit down, that's fine.

- Making aioli by hand is a fun party trick: Get any early arrivals involved in whisking and streaming in the oil.

- Whichever sauce you choose, it can be made 1 day in advance and chilled. If the aioli or tahini solidifies in the fridge, just whisk in a bit of water before serving to loosen it.

> ### For Other Dietary Restrictions
>
> *To serve a vegetarian or vegan guest, roast a whole small-ish eggplant in a 300°F (150°C) oven until it collapses, about an hour, then let cool slightly, pull the skin off, and rub the eggplant in a little bit of harissa, olive oil, salt, and oregano, then spoon some of the roasted sungolds over to serve.*

SLOW-ROASTED HARISSA COD AND SUNGOLDS

For the fish

¼ cup (60 ml) olive oil

3 pounds (1.4 kg) skin-on
   black cod or cod fillets

2 teaspoons kosher salt

¼ cup (64 g) harissa paste

2 tablespoons finely chopped
   fresh oregano

For the sungold sauce

¼ cup (64 g) harissa paste

½ cup (120 ml) olive oil

4 pints (1 kg) sungold
   tomatoes or other cherry
   tomatoes

2 teaspoons kosher salt

SERVES 8, RECIPE EASILY
HALVED TO SERVE 4

Arrange racks in top and center thirds of oven and preheat to 300°F (150°C).

PREP THE FISH

Drizzle the olive oil over a sheet pan, then place the cod, skin side down, on top and season with the salt. Rub the harissa paste evenly all over the cod, then turn to coat in olive oil. Turn back to skin side down and sprinkle with the oregano. If you have room in your fridge and want to get this ready in advance, pop the whole sheet pan of fish into your fridge until you're ready to roast—up to 6 hours in advance—or go ahead and start roasting right away.

PREP THE TOMATOES

In a large shallow baking dish, whisk together the harissa and olive oil, then stir in the tomatoes and season with salt. You can let this sit at room temperature on your counter for up to 2 hours or go ahead and start roasting right away.

Place the tomatoes on the top rack of your oven and the fish on the middle rack. Roast until the fish is opaque and flakes easily when pressed and the tomatoes are bursting and tender. Both should be done in 20 to 30 minutes, but one might finish before the other. The thicker your pieces of fish, the longer they will take to cook—if they're especially thin, start checking them after 15 minutes.

Let the tomatoes sit in the baking dish until ready to serve. As soon as the fish is done, you want to transfer it to a serving platter, so it doesn't overcook on the hot pan. To do so, use a spatula to pull the flesh of the fish off its skin in pieces. This way you get nice skinless portions for serving. Arrange the flaked skinless pieces of fish higgledy piggledy on your serving platter, and then just before serving, spoon the hot sungold sauce over the top. This way the sauce stays warmer and can help warm up the fish just before serving.

CHARRED BROCCOLINI WITH RADICCHIO AND LEMON

2 lemons

2 large or 3 small heads
    radicchio

4 bunches broccolini (about
    2 pounds/910 g)

¼ cup (60 ml) olive oil, plus
    more for serving

Kosher salt and freshly
    ground black pepper

SERVES 8, RECIPE EASILY
HALVED TO SERVE 4

Preheat the oven to 500°F (260°C).

Very thinly slice one of the lemons—a serrated knife is the best tool for this—and remove any seeds. Slice the remaining lemon into wedges and set the wedges aside for serving.

Trim just the very base from the bottom of each head of radicchio and pull off and discard any banged up or wilting outer leaves. Cut into quarters (or even sixths if large) through the stem, then separate the leaves and set aside in a large mixing bowl, covered with a damp clean towel until ready to serve.

Trim the tough bottom stems from the broccolini and slice any piece with a stem thicker than a pencil in half lengthwise through the stem. Transfer to a sheet pan, then toss with the lemon slices and olive oil and season generously with salt and pepper. The prepared sheet pan can sit out at room temperature for 1 hour before roasting, or in the fridge or a cool porch or garage for 3.

Just before you're ready to serve dinner, pop the sheet pan into the top of your hot oven and roast until everything has a hint of char on it, 10 to 15 minutes. Use tongs to transfer the roasted broccolini and lemon wheels to the bowl of radicchio and toss to combine with a generous squeeze of lemon and a drizzle of olive oil. Taste and season as desired with salt and pepper, then transfer to a large serving platter. Drizzle with a bit more olive oil, then nestle a few lemon wedges alongside for squeezing over at the table.

A DINNER OF PORK AND APPLE-BRAISED CABBAGE ON THE GRILL

There are plenty of warm fall days when I still want to cook and entertain outside. This is a menu for one of those days. The whole meal is cooked on the grill, but it is distinctly autumnal. If you've never cooked a pork shoulder steak before, you're going to want to make them all the time once you try this. It's one of my favorite cuts of meat to throw on the grill, but you're probably going to have to special-order it from your butcher or buy a whole boneless pork shoulder and cut it into steaks yourself. A whole pork shoulder fares best slow cooked, but when you slice it into steaks and give it a quick sear on a hot grill it's shockingly tender, juicy, and delightful. It's a relatively quick-to-cook menu—the apples and cabbage can braise in a skillet on the grill while the pork cooks alongside. Buy more fresh apple cider than what you need for the braise and mix it with lemon juice and whiskey to sip while you grill.

Party Size

Serves 4 to 6, recipes easily halved to serve 2 to 3

Party Prep

No advance prep needed; this menu can be cooked and served within an hour or so.

Sauce to Serve
(choose one!)

Pickled Shallot Salsa Verde (page 35)

Pickled Peppercorn Vinaigrette (page 51)

Blender Spiced Green Sauce (page 43)

Optional Add-Ons

A Simple Salad (page 53)

Steamed or boiled potatoes

Bread, toasted on a grill

Special Diets

> ### For Other Dietary Restrictions
>
> *To feed a vegetarian guest, grill a few slabs of Halloumi for them in place of the pork.*
>
> *To feed a vegan or vegetarian guest, grill some large wild mushrooms tossed (separately) in the same spices as the pork, and/or grill some nice thick slices of bread drizzled in olive oil.*

GRILLED SPICED PORK SHOULDER STEAKS

2 teaspoons kosher salt

2 teaspoons brown sugar

2 teaspoons fennel seeds

1 teaspoon cumin seeds

1 teaspoon freshly ground
    black pepper

4 (¾-inch/2-cm thick) pork
    shoulder steaks
    (2 pounds/910 g)

SERVES 4 TO 6, RECIPE
EASILY HALVED TO SERVE
2 TO 3

In a small bowl, stir together the salt, sugar, and spices. Sprinkle evenly on all sides of the pork steaks and let the pork sit on a sheet pan or plate at room temperature at least 30 minutes and up to 1 hour.

Prepare a grill for high-heat grilling. Grill the steaks, turning every minute or two, until lightly charred and crisp and an instant-read thermometer inserted into the thickest part registers 140°F (60°C), 7 to 9 minutes. Transfer the steaks to a cutting board and let rest at least 5 minutes before thinly slicing.

CIDER-BRAISED CABBAGE AND APPLES

3 tablespoons neutral oil, such as sunflower, safflower, or grapeseed, divided

1 green cabbage, cut into 6 wedges through the center of the core (to hold each wedge together)

Kosher salt and freshly ground black pepper

1 pound (455 g) apples, preferably small Pink Lady apples, halved through the core

2 cups (480 ml) fresh apple cider

2 tablespoons cold unsalted butter, cut into cubes

Juice of ½ lemon

SERVES 4 TO 6, RECIPE EASILY HALVED TO SERVE 2 TO 3

Prepare a grill for high-heat grilling. In a 12-inch (30.5-cm) cast-iron skillet, swirl 2 tablespoons of the oil, then place on the grill and heat until smoking. Add the cabbage wedges in a single layer and cook until charred on one side, then season generously with salt and pepper and flip.

While the second side of the cabbage wedges char, toss the apples in the remaining 1 tablespoon of oil, then arrange cut side down on the grates of the grill and cook just until lightly charred, 2 to 3 minutes. Transfer to the skillet with the cabbage. Add the cider and braise until the cabbage and apples are tender and the cider has reduced quite a bit, 15 to 25 minutes. Remove from the heat and transfer the cabbage and apples to a serving platter, leaving the braising liquid behind in the skillet. Add the butter and lemon juice to the liquid left in the skillet and swirl until melted to emulsify the sauce. Taste, then season with salt and pepper if needed. Pour the sauce over the cabbage and apples and serve immediately.

A TOTALLY FESTIVE WAY TO SERVE BEANS FOR DINNER

When there are too many different dietary restrictions around one table, beans and rice and sweet potatoes and winter squash will (almost) always feed everyone. Soupy pinto beans cooked from scratch with extra fussing will become everyone's favorite dish on the table. It helps to seek out the best quality, freshest dried pinto beans you can find. (I love Rancho Gordo beans.) Spoon the soupy beans over rice and drizzle everything with creamy jalapeño sauce. Add some double-roasted sweet potatoes and squash on the side, and maybe some fresh greens, and it's special-occasion worthy. Double-roasting winter squash and sweet potatoes is one of my favorite do-ahead time savers. You don't have to peel or cut anything: Roast the potatoes and squash whole until tender, then they're easy to tear open into pieces with your hands. Brush with butter, season with salt, and roast until they're warm and crisped, then serve them topped with spicy hot buttered nuts.

Party Size
Serves 8 to 10, recipes easily halved to serve 4 to 5

Party Prep
At least 1 day of advance prep is required, and up to 5 days of advance prep is allowed.

Sauces to Serve
Creamy Jalapeño Sauce (page 38)

Pickled Onions (page 44)

Optional Add-Ons
Rice

Shredded (thinly sliced) romaine or baby arugula, undressed, for adding to tacos

Special Diets

PLANNING ADVICE

- The pickled onions can be made up to 5 days in advance.

- The beans can be made up to 3 days ahead of serving. Either way, make sure to soak them overnight before cooking.

- The sweet potatoes and squash can be roasted up to 1 day in advance, but don't tear them yet—let cool and then refrigerate in an airtight container. Tear and arrange them on a sheet pan ready to be roasted up to 1 hour before your guests arrive, and then roast them 10 minutes before you're ready to serve.

- Make the brown butter sauce up to 1 hour and at least 10 minutes before serving.

- The creamy jalapeño sauce is best made the same day it's served, but you can make it a few hours in advance.

> ### For Other Dietary Restrictions
>
> *To feed a dairy-free or vegan guest, use coconut oil instead of butter for the nuts. The coconut oil won't brown the same as butter, but it will still taste amazing.*

DOUBLE-ROASTED SWEET POTATOES AND
KABOCHA SQUASH WITH HOT BUTTERED NUTS

3 pounds (1.4 kg) purple
sweet potatoes (or garnet
yams if you can't find
purple sweet potatoes)

2 kabocha squash

¾ cup (1½ sticks/170 g) plus
2 tablespoons butter,
divided

½ cup (60 g) raw pumpkin
seeds

½ cup (60 g) coarsely
chopped pecans

1 tablespoon Aleppo-style
pepper flakes

Kosher salt

Juice of ½ lemon

SERVES 8 TO 10, RECIPE
EASILY HALVED TO SERVE
4 TO 5

Heat the oven to 400°F (205°C).

Poke the potatoes and squash here and there with a fork, then place on a sheet pan and roast until they give easily when pressed with your finger, about 1 hour. Remove from the oven and let cool until cool enough to handle, then place in a container and pop them in the fridge or stash in a cool garage or porch if serving tomorrow, or let them hang out on the counter for a few hours if serving today.

Make the brown butter sauce up to 1 hour and at least 10 minutes before serving: In a large cold skillet, place ¾ cup (170 g) of the butter, seeds, and nuts and warm over medium heat until the butter is melted. Continue cooking, stirring often, until the butter, seeds, and nuts are all lightly browned and the whole skillet smells toasted and caramelized, 6 to 8 minutes. Remove from the heat and stir in the Aleppo-style pepper flakes and 1 teaspoon of salt. If making in advance, you're going to have to rewarm this right before serving.

Before your guests arrive, use your hands to tear the sweet potatoes open into about 4-inch (10-cm) pieces and arrange them skin side down on a sheet pan. Tear open the kabocha squash, scoop out and discard the seeds, then tear each one into small boats and arrange skin side down on the sheet pan with the sweet potatoes. You might need a second sheet pan to fit everything. Don't crowd the pieces; you want them all to have plenty of room to roast. Set the sheet pans aside until about 10 minutes before you're ready to serve dinner.

Heat your broiler to high. Melt the remaining 2 tablespoons of butter and brush that over the tops of the potatoes and squash boats, then season the whole lot with salt. Working one tray at a time, broil until the tops of the squash and sweet potato pieces are lightly charred, about 5 minutes. Transfer to a serving platter, and top with the hot buttered nuts and seeds (re-warm first if needed), then squeeze lemon juice over the top and serve immediately.

SOUPY SPICED PINTO BEANS

1 pound (453 g) pinto beans, rinsed

2 tablespoons plus ½ cup (120 ml) olive oil, divided

1 onion, halved through the root (not peeled)

1 whole head garlic, halved crosswise (not peeled)

2 dried New Mexico chiles, wiped clean

1 tablespoon double-concentrated tomato paste

2 bay leaves

1 strip kombu (optional, but this seaweed supposedly helps make beans more digestible)

Kosher salt

1 teaspoon apple cider vinegar

SERVES 8 TO 10, RECIPE
EASILY HALVED TO SERVE
4 TO 5

Soak the beans in water overnight.

Up to 3 days before serving, cook the beans. In a large heavy pot or Dutch oven, heat 2 tablespoons of the oil over medium until shimmering. Sear the onion and garlic, cut sides down, until deeply browned, about 4 minutes. Add the chiles and tomato paste and cook until fragrant, 1 to 2 minutes. Add the beans and cover with water by 2 inches (5 cm). Add the bay leaves and kombu (if using) and 1 tablespoon of salt and stir to combine. Pour the remaining ½ cup (120 ml) olive oil over the top. Bring to a boil, then reduce the heat to a simmer and partially cover.

Continue to cook, stirring every once in a while, until the beans are tender but still hold their shape, 2 to 3 hours. The time it takes for the beans to cook will really depend on the freshness of your beans. This is why I like to always cook beans at least a day before serving them, in case they take a lot longer than expected.

Remove from the heat and fish out and discard the onion, garlic, bay leaves, and kombu. Stir in the vinegar and now taste your beans. If they need more salt (and they probably do), add some. Chill the beans in their cooking liquid until ready to serve.

Before serving, bring the beans and their cooking liquid to a boil, uncovered, then transfer to a serving bowl or platter with as little or as much of their cooking liquid as you like.

A COZY BRAISED CHICKEN AND SALAD DINNER

The Silver Palate cookbook was one of my mom's favorites in the nineties, and I cooked from it often with her. When I moved into my first apartment after college, it was the first cookbook I bought myself. And I'm pretty sure Chicken Marbella was what I served at my first dinner party in that apartment, except I always made it with chicken thighs because they're my favorite. Over the years my take on that classic entrée has evolved, and it now includes white beans, because white beans are my favorite food to saturate with chicken fat. All that braised chicken and beans and prunes and olives need something bitter to balance it out, and you can absolutely serve it with a simple arugula or escarole salad, but I like to serve it with a salad of Lacinato kale and radicchio sliced into ribbons. This is a cozy and easy oven-to-table menu, equally suited for entertaining or your Wednesday night family dinner. Repeat it often until it's spring.

Party Size

4 to 6, recipes easily doubled to serve 8 to 10 or halved to serve 2 to 3

Party Prep

Some advance prep is required. The whole menu can be cooked in about 1½ hours; some of the prep can be done the morning before.

Sauce to Serve

Gremolata (page 47)

Optional Add-Ons

Bread

Special Diets

PLANNING ADVICE

- If doubling the recipes, you're going to want to braise the chicken in two baking dishes or a very large roasting pan.

- You can assemble the braise the morning before cooking.

- The chicken cooks for about 1 hour in the oven, so be sure to put it in to braise at least 1 hour and 15 minutes before you want to sit down to eat.

- Slicing salad ribbons, making salad dressing, and massaging the salad are good group activities, so feel free to do that prep with guests when they arrive—no need to have it done in advance.

- Make the gremolata no more than 1 hour in advance so that it doesn't get wilty and weird.

For Other Dietary Restrictions

If serving a pescatarian guest, you can make a small version of the braised chicken with a thick cod fillet. Add all the same ingredients and cook just until the cod is opaque and the layers of flesh separate easily when pressed, 5 to 10 minutes depending on thickness.

If serving a vegetarian or vegan guest, you can make them a just-beans version in a smaller baking dish, just increase the amount of beans.

BRAISED CHICKEN THIGHS WITH WHITE BEANS, PRUNES, AND OLIVES

8 to 12 small chicken thighs
(2.5 to 3 pounds/1.2 to
1.4 kg)

2 teaspoons kosher salt

1 teaspoon freshly ground
black pepper

4 cloves garlic, grated

1 tablespoon olive oil

2 tablespoons sherry vinegar

3 (15.5-ounce/439-g) cans
white beans, drained and
rinsed

1 cup pitted prunes

1 cup pitted green olives

¼ cup (30 g) capers, drained

¼ cup (60 ml) dry white wine

SERVES 4 TO 6, RECIPE
EASILY DOUBLED TO SERVE
8 TO 10 OR HALVED TO
SERVE 2 TO 3

Place the chicken thighs in a large baking dish. Season on all sides with salt and pepper. Add the garlic, oil, and vinegar and toss to coat. Add the white beans, prunes, olives, and capers and pull the chicken thighs, skin side up, to the top, nestling everything in an even layer, then pour the wine over. You can let this sit at room temperature for up to 20 minutes before braising, or cover and pop the whole thing in the fridge or in a safe cold place (below 40°F [4.5°C] and above 32°F [0°C]) for up to 8 hours before braising.

When ready to cook, arrange a rack in the top third of your oven and preheat to 400°F (205°C). You want the chicken to braise in the top of your oven because it'll help the skin be closer to the heat so it has a chance to get nice and crispy.

Roast on the top rack until the chicken is cooked through and the skin is browned, 45 to 60 minutes. Transfer to a serving platter or serve it directly out of the baking dish—either way, let it cool about 10 minutes before serving, since this dish holds a lot of heat and you don't want anyone to burn themselves.

BITTER RIBBONS SALAD

2 bunches Lacinato kale

1 large or 2 small heads
   radicchio

2 tablespoons olive oil

2 tablespoons lemon juice

1 tablespoon honey

1 teaspoon Aleppo-style
   pepper flakes

½ teaspoon kosher salt

SERVES 4 TO 6, RECIPE EASILY
DOUBLED TO SERVE 8 TO 10
OR HALVED TO SERVE 2 TO 3

Remove the stems from each leaf of kale. Working in batches of 4 to 6 leaves at a time, stack the leaves and roll them up lengthwise into a log, then thinly slice the log crosswise to create ribbons of kale. Transfer to a large salad or mixing bowl.

Trim and discard the stems and outer leaves of the radicchio, then cut in half lengthwise though the stem. Place each half flat side down on a cutting board and thinly slice, then transfer to the bowl with the kale.

At this point you can cover your bowl of bitter ribbons with a clean, cold damp dish towel and let sit at room temperature for up to 1 hour. That cold, damp towel will help keep the greens fresh without having to take up room in the fridge.

In a small bowl, whisk together the olive oil, lemon juice, honey, Aleppo, and salt until smooth. Dip a piece of kale in to taste it, and add more salt or honey if desired. Set aside until ready to toss the salad.

Up to 30 minutes before serving, pour the dressing over the bowl of ribbons, and use your hands to toss and massage the greens. Just like a good massage helps loosen your shoulders, massaging raw kale helps loosen and relax the cell structure of the leaves so they're easier to chew and digest. Don't be shy with massaging: You want to really squeeze and rub until the kale turns shiny and darker in color and everything is evenly coated in dressing. Transfer to a serving platter if desired or keep in the salad bowl.

A SHEET-PAN MEATBALLS AND ROASTED SQUASH DINNER

We should all be roasting grapes more often. Their sweetness intensifies, they get softer, and, you know, *hot*, which is good for cold weather. I like to pile them over roasted delicata squash rings. It's a lot of sweet things, but so very cozy and fun—just don't forget to squeeze some lemon juice over the top to balance it all out. Earthy, spicy, merguez-inspired meatballs are an excellent match, swimming in a pool of cool garlicky yogurt sauce. And for the clean-stovetop-obsessed among us, this whole menu cooks in the oven. And you can even form the meatballs and prep the squash rings in advance, so the whole menu magically happens in the oven while you sip a martini with your guests.

Party Size
Serves 6 to 8, recipes easily halved to serve 3 to 4

Party Prep
Some advance prep is required, but the whole menu cooks in the oven in less than an hour.

Sauce to Serve (choose one or both!)
Garlicky Yogurt Sauce (page 32)

Gremolata (made with pistachios, page 47)

Optional Add-Ons
Bread or Skillet Socca (page 28)

A Simple Salad (page 53)

Rice or quinoa

Special Diets

PLANNING ADVICE

- The meatball mixture can be made up to 2 days in advance, and the meatballs can be formed up to 1 day in advance. Cover and refrigerate until ready to roast.

- The yogurt sauce can be made 1 day in advance and chilled.

- For this menu, make the gremolata with pistachios if you have them, and make it no more than 1 hour in advance so that it doesn't get wilty and weird.

- If you only have one oven, roast the squash and grapes first, then pop the meatballs in to roast quickly right after—the meatballs are best piping hot, while the squash doesn't mind being room temperature. If you have two ovens, of course go ahead and roast them at the same time.

- If serving with socca, make it first and don't worry about serving it warm—you want the meatballs to be the last thing out of the oven.

For Other Dietary Restrictions

To serve a dairy-free guest, keep the yogurt sauce on the side or forgo the sauce entirely and serve Tahini Sauce (page 42) instead.

To serve a vegetarian guest, reserve a bit of the harissa-spice mixture before you add the lamb to it and use it to toss with carrots and chickpeas. Roast the carrots and chickpeas together in a 450°F (230°C) oven until the carrots are tender and the chickpeas are crisped, about 15 to 20 minutes, then serve on a separate plate over yogurt and top with gremolata.

OVEN LAMB MEATBALLS

3 teaspoons coriander seeds

2 teaspoons cumin seeds

¼ cup (64 g) harissa paste

2 teaspoons kosher salt

2 teaspoons ground
cinnamon

2 pounds (910 g) ground
lamb (you can use beef,
if you can't find lamb or
prefer it)

2 tablespoons olive oil

SERVES 6 TO 8, RECIPE
EASILY HALVED TO SERVE
3 TO 4

In a small skillet, heat the coriander seeds and cumin seeds over medium, stirring often, until fragrant, about 4 minutes. Remove from the heat and let cool. Coarsely grind in a spice grinder or mortar and pestle, then transfer to a large bowl. Add the harissa paste, salt, and cinnamon, and stir to combine. Add the lamb and use your hands to work the spice mixture into the meat until well combined. At this point the mixture can be chilled for up to 2 days until ready to roast or formed into meatballs up to 1 day before roasting.

To form meatballs: Rub a sheet pan with olive oil. With olive oil on your hands to keep the meat mixture from sticking to you, form 2½-inch (6-cm) balls (a little larger than a golf ball) and place about 1 inch (2.5 cm) apart on the oiled sheet pan. You should get about 24 balls, and they should all fit on one sheet pan. (If halving the recipe, you can use a quarter sheet.) At this point you can cover the sheet pan of balls and stash it in the fridge or a safe cold place (below 40°F [4.5°C] and above 32°F [0°C]) for up to 1 day, until ready to roast and serve.

When almost ready to serve, crank the oven to 500°F (260°C). Roast the meatballs on the top rack of the oven until lightly browned on top and firm but still juicy, 8 to 10 minutes. Cut one open to make sure it's done: You want the inside to be pink and juicy like a good burger, not purple and raw.

If serving with the yogurt sauce, swoosh the sauce over the surface of a serving platter. Arrange the meatballs on top (or on the platter if skipping the yogurt sauce or serving it on the side), then spoon the flavorful oil left in the sheet pan over the tops of the meatballs. Top with pistachio gremolata, and serve immediately.

ROASTED GRAPES AND DELICATA SQUASH RINGS

2 large or 3 small delicata
squash (about 3
pounds/1.4 kg total)
¼ cup (60 ml) olive oil, plus
more for serving
1 pound (455 g) seedless
grapes on the vine,
preferably black
Kosher salt and freshly
ground black pepper
Juice of ½ lemon, for serving
Flaky sea salt, for serving

SERVES 6 TO 8, RECIPE
EASILY HALVED TO SERVE
3 TO 4

Preheat the oven to 450°F (230°C).

Cut the squash in half crosswise, scoop out the seeds with a small spoon, then slice into ¼-inch (6-mm) rings. Toss with 2 tablespoons of the olive oil and season with salt and pepper, then spread in a single layer on a sheet pan. You might need two sheet pans for this; you want to make sure all the rings are flat on the sheet pan. Roast until the bottoms are crisp and golden brown, 15 to 20 minutes.

Meanwhile, in a large ovenproof skillet, heat the remaining 2 tablespoons of oil. Use scissors to snip the bunch of grapes into small clusters, then add the grape clusters to the hot oil in the skillet and season with salt and pepper. Toss to combine, then transfer to the oven and roast until the grapes begin to burst and shrivel, about 10 minutes.

Transfer the squash rings and grapes to a serving platter. Drizzle with olive oil, squeeze lemon juice over, then sprinkle with flaky salt and serve.

A BETTER WAY TO SERVE ROASTED VEGETABLES AND LENTILS FOR DINNER

Cauliflower and mushrooms should always have crispy edges—they're just better that way. But the usual stovetop ways to get them there are a bother when cooking for a crowd. Instead, I crank my oven up and get them crispy on sheet pans with a little help from lots of olive oil and some Parmesan cheese. They should be roasted separately, but I love the way these two vegetables combine on the plate: mild and sweet while assertive and musky, and swiped through a creamy sauce. To go with all that roasty toastiness, a warm lentil salad packed with tons of dill is just the thing. To give my lentils a punch of flavor I sizzle lemon zest, coriander seeds, and a whole bunch of sliced green onions in lots of olive oil, then I pour it into the lentils. Honestly that oil is so good you'll want to make it again for other things, like pouring over a whole bunch of freshly grilled vegetables in the summer. But it's fall right now, and this menu is a good mix of cozy and fresh.

Party Size

Serves 4 to 6, recipes easily halved to serve 2 to 3

Party Prep

Best cooked right before serving, but some advance prep can be done.

Sauce to Serve
(choose one!)

Aioli (page 41)

Tahini Sauce (page 42)

Garlicky Yogurt Sauce (page 32)

Optional Add-Ons

Bread or Skillet Socca (page 28)

Greens tossed in Pickled Peppercorn Vinaigrette (page 51)

Special Diets

PLANNING ADVICE

- The lentils can be made about 1 hour before your guests arrive then re-warmed just before serving. If doing so, don't add the dill until after you re-warm them.

- The mushrooms and cauliflower are going to need to be roasted while your guests are there, but you can assemble the sheet pans before they arrive, then pop them in the hot oven 30 minutes before you're ready to sit down to eat so they're hot and crispy when you serve them.

- Whichever sauce you choose, it can be made 1 day in advance and chilled. If the aioli solidifies in the fridge, just whisk in a bit of water before serving to loosen it.

> ### For Other Dietary Restrictions
>
> *If serving a vegan or dairy-free guest, skip the Parm on the cauliflower. It won't get as crispy, but it'll still be good. Just add some extra salt since the Parm is so salty.*
>
> *If serving a vegan guest, don't serve aioli or yogurt as your creamy sauce option.*
>
> *If serving a dairy-free guest, don't serve yogurt sauce as your creamy sauce option.*

CRISPY ROASTED CAULIFLOWER AND MUSHROOMS

1 large head cauliflower

1 pound (455 g) maitake mushrooms

7 tablespoons (105 ml) olive oil, divided

1 teaspoon freshly ground black pepper

6 thyme sprigs

¾ cup (70 g) finely grated Parmesan cheese

2 teaspoons kosher salt

1½ teaspoons crushed red pepper flakes

Flaky salt, for serving

SERVES 4 TO 6, RECIPE EASILY HALVED TO SERVE 2 TO 3

Preheat the oven to 450°F (230°C).

Cut the cauliflower in half through the core, then lay each half down flat on a cutting board and slice it crosswise into 1-inch (2.5-cm) planks. Trim the tough bottoms of the mushrooms off, then gently tear into 2-inch (5-cm) pieces with your hands.

On a sheet pan, toss the mushrooms with 4 tablespoons (60 ml) of the olive oil. Season with 1 teaspoon pepper—but not salt. (Salt the mushrooms at the end of cooking to help them crisp better!) Scatter the thyme sprigs over the top.

Pour the remaining 3 tablespoons of olive oil on a second sheet pan and add the cauliflower, gently tossing to coat without breaking your nice big flat pieces. Sprinkle half the Parmesan, salt, and red pepper flakes over the top, then flip all the pieces and sprinkle the remaining half over the top.

Roast the mushrooms and cauliflower, rotating the sheet pans once halfway through, until the mushrooms are golden-brown and crispy and the cauliflower is fork-tender with a nice golden brown crust, about 30 minutes. The mushrooms might finish before your cauliflower, so start checking them at 20 minutes.

Combine the mushrooms and cauliflower on a (preferably warm) platter and sprinkle with flaky salt to serve.

LEMON-DILL LENTILS

2 cups (380 g) green
(French) or black (beluga)
lentils, rinsed

Kosher salt

1 sprig fresh thyme

1 cup olive oil

1 bunch green onions, thinly
sliced (green and white
parts)

2 teaspoons coriander seeds

Zest and juice of 2 lemons

1 bunch dill, finely chopped

SERVES 4 TO 6, RECIPE
EASILY HALVED TO SERVE
2 TO 3

Place the lentils in a pot and cover by 2 inches (5 cm) with water. Salt generously, add the thyme, and bring to a boil over medium-high. Reduce the heat to a simmer and continue to cook until the lentils are al dente (bite one to find out: You want them to be soft enough to easily bite and chew, but not soft enough to mush), about 12 minutes. Drain, and return to the pot.

Meanwhile, in a large cold skillet, stir the oil, green onions, coriander seeds, and lemon zest. Heat over medium, swirling occasionally, until the green onions have stopped sizzling and have started to lightly brown, and the oil is deeply fragrant, about 10 minutes. Remove from the heat, stir in the lemon juice, and pour over the cooked lentils. You want to pour this oil over the lentils while both are still warm because the flavors will absorb better that way. At this point you can cover and let sit in the pot for up to 2 hours at room temperature. Before serving, re-warm if necessary over medium heat, stirring. Have a taste and add more salt if needed. Stir in the chopped dill, then transfer to a serving platter.

GAMES FOR THE TABLE (AND PARLOR)

WHISPER DOWN THE LANE

Some people call it Telephone, but my family has always called it Whisper Down the Lane, and we played it around every holiday dinner table. The wider the age range at the table, the more hilarious the game. We never could figure out if Grandma couldn't hear us or was just pulling our legs when she changed the phrase as she whispered it to the next person, but I suspect it was a mixture of both. Anyway, this is a very easy, very silly game to play during a dinner party, especially suited to gatherings of more than ten with some kids in the mix. Here's how: One person starts by whispering a phrase (anything they like!) into the ear of their neighbor to the right. Then that person whispers it into the ear of their neighbor to the right and so on and so forth until the message reaches the person seated to the left of whoever started it. This guest says the phrase they heard out loud to the whole table, and then the guest who started the round announces their phrase to the table. It is very important, if you are the person to start a round, to remember exactly what you said! Ideally, the difference is hilarious, but not incomprehensible. Some guidelines to keep in mind while you play: Continue conversation and chatter while each whisper is passed so you don't hear the phrase until it comes to you. You may only ask to have a phrase repeated to you by your neighbor once.

MUSICAL CHAIRS

When faced with a crowd of ten or more at the table, and even when not, it can help keep the conversation lively if you switch up who you're sitting next to at least once during the night. If you'd like to do so, announce at the beginning of the meal that you'll be playing musical chairs at dinner tonight. Except not really, because in the game of musical chairs a chair is always taken away and someone loses a spot. And that's just not in the inclusive spirit of a dinner party, is it? When the moment feels right, clink your glass, and announce it's time to switch places! Everyone must grab their plate, utensils, and glasses (careful, it's a lot to carry—you might need to make two trips!) and move to a new seat at the table. You, as the host, can stay put if you like. This is a bit of a shuffle-production, so it's really only necessary to do once or twice during the course of the night. For less shuffle-production, proclaim it's time to switch seats just once, between dinner and dessert as plates are cleared.

CHARADES

Come to enough dinner parties at my house and chances are you will play charades. It is my favorite after-dinner game. But to get people geared up to play before getting too cozy and lazy lounging after dinner, I start it at the table. There are many ways to play this game, but I like it without timers and without keeping score, because the true fun of the game is in the process. But what if it takes one person ten minutes to act out a clue before their team guesses it, you ask? Lean into the process and you'll see that sometimes the longer it takes, the more bizarre, creative, and relationship-bonding this game can get. Here's how I play charades:

1. Divide the table into two equal teams. You decide how to do this. Sometimes I break up couples between teams, sometimes I don't. Sometimes the easiest thing to do is one side of the table vs. the other side. I do try to make sure that each team has at least one person on it who has played with me before.

2. Give each team a bowl full of strips of paper (around twenty strips will usually suffice) and a few pens, then send one team away into the living room to write their clues while one team stays at the table to write theirs.

3. Write one clue on each strip of paper, coming up with each clue together as a team. Everyone should know every clue their team writes, so that they can enjoy watching the other team members tackle each one while knowing what they're trying to act out.

4. What should your clues be? Well, the way I play it, anything goes! Traditionally charades stick to categories like movies, books, songs, people, or places, but I like to be a little more whimsical than that. A reference from the party is always a fun inside joke, like "Anna's Magic Wine Stain Remover," or it could be a made-up thing like "Nativity Scene After an Earthquake" or simply a concept, like "Communism." Think about what you want to see the people on the other team try to act out, and then be creative. Tailor your clues to the crowd of people you are playing with.

5. Once the clues are all written, gather in the living room or back at the table—wherever you have space for everyone to sit. Clear an area to be "the stage" and make sure each team sits together.

6. To play, each team alternates performing and guessing. There's no repeat turns if you win here because there's no winning.

7. For each turn, one team member gets up and draws a clue out of the bowl of the opposite team. Pass the clue to the opposite team so they can judge you (with love), then face your team and start trying to make them guess what the clue is. No talking and no props are allowed. Hold up your fingers to show how many words it is, then start acting. To act out one word at a time, hold up your fingers to show which word in the phrase you're acting out. If you don't know how to act out a word but there's a word that sounds like it that you can act out, tug at your ear to indicate "sounds like," then act that out until your team guesses the word.

8. If and when a team member is struggling too much by themselves "on stage," it is perfectly acceptable for someone from the opposite team to get up and help if needed. Remember, this is not a competition, just a game to be played together for fun.

9. Continue playing until everyone is tired of laughing, is getting too drunk to make sense anymore, or has finished all the clues in all the bowls.

WINTER

WINTER MENUS

Slow roasts, long braises . . . basically the longer dinner is in the oven or on the stove right now the better. I'm not sorry for the fact that three out of my six winter menus that follow contain potatoes. 'Tis the season. It's also the season for more wine and dairy in my cooking, because snowy cold winter is the time for dinner parties that feel like a cozy hug and an elegant European vacation all at once. None of these menus are specifically holiday menus, but they all work great for any holiday or occasion you celebrate in the winter.

A ROASTED LEG OF LAMB AND POTATOES DINNER

Smoked Spanish paprika (pimentón) is the fairy dust in my spice drawer. It makes everything better, and I reach for it (perhaps too) often. A high-quality, fresh jar is worth seeking out and using liberally. I love the one sold by Burlap & Barrel—it adds a rich savory depth and smokiness to everything it touches (just like bacon). In this menu I use it to toss with the crispy roasted potatoes as a loving salute to Spanish patatas bravas. In another tapas-inspired move, I roast marinated artichoke hearts until super crispy to add to those potatoes. Artichokes and potatoes are both excellent dragged through lots of aioli. You may want to make the potatoes again in a smaller quantity as a cocktail snack someday, but here we're making them for a crowd with a boneless leg of lamb roasted, sliced, and doused in an orange pan sauce full of salty black olives. It's punchy and bright and cozy and warm and celebratory.

Party Size	Sauce to Serve	Special Diets
Serves 10 to 12	Aioli (double the recipe for this one—page 41)	
Party Prep	**Optional Add-Ons**	
One day advance prep is required, as is some last-minute cooking.	Arugula or escarole salad dressed with Lemony Vinaigrette (page 48)	

PLANNING ADVICE

- For best flavor, the lamb should be marinated overnight.

- If you don't have butcher's twine, ask your butcher for just enough for the lamb when you pick it up. They're always happy to give it to you for free with a roast.

- The aioli can be made 1 day in advance and chilled. If it solidifies in the fridge, just whisk in a bit of water before serving to loosen it.

- Potatoes can be parboiled and chilled in an airtight container or bag up to 2 days in advance.

- If you don't get around to prepping the potatoes before your guests arrive, put them to work peeling and chopping potatoes while the lamb is in the oven—it's a fun group activity.

- As soon as the lamb comes out of the oven, it's time to crank up the oven to roast the potatoes and artichoke hearts. Don't slice the lamb until the potatoes are done.

For Other Dietary Restrictions

To serve a vegetarian or vegan guest, roast some broccolini tossed in olive oil, salt, pepper, chopped rosemary, grated orange zest, and garlic in a 500°F oven (260°C) oven until lightly charred, about 10 minutes, and serve that in place of lamb.

If serving a dairy-free guest, save them some lamb without the pan sauce on it.

If serving a vegan guest, offer them some storebought vegan mayonnaise for their broccolini in place of the aioli.

LAMB ROAST WITH OLIVES AND ORANGES

1 orange

8 anchovy fillets

6 cloves garlic

¼ cup (60 ml) olive oil,
plus 2 tablespoons for
the skillet

1 tablespoon fresh rosemary

1 tablespoon kosher salt

1 (4 to 5-pound/1.8 to 2.3-kg)
butterflied boneless lamb
leg roast, untied

1 cup (155 g) oil-cured pitted
olives

1 cup (240 ml) dry white wine

4 tablespoons cold butter,
cut into pieces

White wine vinegar, if needed

SERVES 10 TO 12

Zest the orange and add the zest to the jar of a (preferably mini) food processor, reserving the orange. Pulse the zest with the anchovies, garlic, ¼ cup (60 ml) olive oil, rosemary, and salt until a paste forms. Use your hands (apologies, but this scent will linger—feel free to don gloves if you're worried about that) to rub this paste all over the butterflied leg of lamb, then roll it up into a tight cylinder "roast" and tie it tightly around the circumference at regular intervals with butcher's twine. Cover and chill overnight for best flavor, or for at least 4 hours. Let come to room temperature before cooking.

Preheat the oven to 375°F (190°C).

Slice the zested orange into ¼-inch (6-mm) slices. In a large cast iron or ovenproof skillet, heat the 2 tablespoons of olive oil over medium-high. Sear the lamb roast, turning occasionally, until all sides are deeply golden brown, about 12 minutes. Add the orange slices and olives to the skillet and transfer to the oven to roast, turning the lamb once halfway through, until an instant-read thermometer inserted in the center reads 140°F (60°C), about 1 hour. Transfer to a cutting board and let rest 15 to 30 minutes before slicing, reserving the orange slices and olives in the skillet. Don't forget to remove the butcher's twine before slicing!

Meanwhile, set the skillet on the stove over medium heat and deglaze with the wine, scraping up any browned bits off the bottom. Once the wine has reduced by half, turn off the heat, add the butter, and swirl until the butter is melted and the sauce is emulsified. Taste and add a tiny splash of vinegar if it needs more acidity, or a sprinkle of salt if it needs more salt. On a serving platter, drizzle sauce, olives, and oranges over sliced lamb.

CRISPIEST ROASTED POTATOES AND ARTICHOKES

5 pounds (2.3 kg) russet
    potatoes, peeled and cut
    into 1½- to 2-inch (4- to
    5-cm) pieces
¼ cup (60 ml) sherry vinegar
    or apple cider vinegar
Kosher salt
½ cup (120 ml) olive oil,
    divided
½ cup (120 ml) neutral
    oil, such as sunflower,
    safflower, or grapeseed
    oil, divided
4 (12-oz/340-g) jars
    marinated artichoke
    hearts, drained
1 tablespoon smoked paprika

SERVES 10 TO 12, EASILY
HALVED TO SERVE 5 TO 6

Place the potatoes in a pot and cover by 2 inches (5 cm) with water. Stir in the vinegar and 2 tablespoons of kosher salt and heat over high until boiling, then reduce to low heat and continue to cook until the potatoes are tender on the outside but still firm inside, about 12 minutes. Strain and let cool to room temperature. You can now either refrigerate the parboiled potatoes in an airtight container or bag for up to 2 days or proceed with roasting.

Preheat the oven to 500°F (260°C).

Divide both oils equally between two sheet pans and add the potatoes to one and the artichoke hearts to the other, then toss to coat well. Set the artichoke sheet pan aside and roast the potatoes on the top rack of the oven until the bottom sides are golden brown and crisp, 15 to 20 minutes. Remove the potatoes from the oven, use a fish spatula or other thin metal spatula to flip them, then return them to the oven along with the sheet pan of artichokes and continue to roast until the artichokes are browned and crisped and the potatoes are golden brown and crisp all over, 10 to 15 minutes. Sprinkle the potatoes with paprika and 1 teaspoon of salt and toss to coat, then transfer the potatoes and artichoke hearts to a serving platter and toss to combine.

A DUCK BREAST AND BITTER ORANGE SALAD DINNER

A whole platter of sliced duck breast, each pink slice crowned with golden-brown crisp skin, is pure and simple love and decadence. You should cook duck breast more often—it's really not as hard as you might think, and though it's a bird, it eats like a steak. I've got a trick for you here to help you cook it almost entirely in advance, so you're not watching the stove while hosting. To go with it, let's sing a song of praise to citrus season. The fact that we can eat fresh and bright sweet-tart globes of citrus in the winter even in the chilly dark Northeast is a miracle of the modern world. Just when we need that sunshine the most, oranges deliver. I love them best tossed with something bitter, like escarole, which I really could eat all winter long. I first served this flirty menu at a Valentine's Day dinner party, and so I always think of it as a feast of love, no matter the occasion.

Party Size
Serves 4 to 6, recipes easily doubled to serve 8 to 12 or halved to serve 2 to 3

Party Prep
The full menu can be prepped and served within an hour or two.

Sauce to Serve
(choose one or two)
Aioli (page 41)

Blender Spiced Green Sauce (page 43)

Pickled Peppercorn Vinaigrette (page 51)

Optional Add-Ons
Bread or Skillet Socca (page 28)

Special Diets

PLANNING ADVICE

- You can prep your escarole and make a sauce up to 1 day in advance. Aioli can solidify when chilled, so just whisk in a bit of water before serving to loosen it.

- The pickled onions can be made up to 5 days in advance.

- The duck breasts can be scored and rendered up to 1 hour in advance. Set them aside at room temperature until ready to sear and serve.

For Other Dietary Restrictions

To serve a vegetarian or vegan guest, slice trumpet mushrooms into thick coins (they'll look kind of like scallops) and sear them over medium-high heat in olive oil until crisp on both sides, about 10 minutes total, then season with salt, pepper, and just a tiny bit of ground allspice. Or slice them into slabs and cross-hatch both sides before searing the same way and they'll be even closer in texture and presentation to the duck.

To serve a pescatarian, a few large scallops seared in butter will do quite nicely.

CRISPY-SKINNED SLICED DUCK BREAST

4 duck breasts (about 4
   pounds/1.8 kg)
2 teaspoons kosher salt
2 teaspoons freshly ground
   black pepper, plus more
   for serving
½ teaspoon ground allspice
Flaky sea salt, for serving

SERVES 4 TO 6, RECIPE
EASILY DOUBLED TO SERVE
8 TO 12 OR HALVED TO
SERVE 2 TO 3

Using your sharpest knife, score the skin on each duck breast in a diagonal pattern. This is going to help the fat render more completely to give you crispier skin. To do this, start on one side of the breast and gently slice diagonally across the fat, cutting down to just before you reach the dark meat. Repeat in parallel diagonal lines about ¼ inch (6 mm) apart all the way across, then turn the breast and slice in the other direction, so you have even, little squares of duck fat all across the top. Don't rush this process, especially if it's your first time doing it. Once all the breasts are scored, stir together the salt, pepper, and allspice in a small bowl and season each breast on all sides with the mixture.

In two large (cold!) skillets, place the seasoned breasts skin side down. You want to give each breast a lot of room to breathe, because there's going to be a lot of fat coming off them soon. Heat both skillets over the lowest possible heat your stove can muster. You want the duck to slowly warm up with the skillet, so that the fat has more time to render before starting to crisp. Don't rush this process. Continue to cook on the lowest possible heat, checking the underside to make sure it's not getting too dark by gently nudging it up with tongs, until the breasts are swimming in fat and the skin side is lightly golden brown. This should take anywhere from 10 to 20 minutes, depending on how fatty your duck is and how strong your stove is. If your stove is too strong to slowly render fat, turn it off and let the heat of the pan work on its own, turning it on and off as needed to keep it cooking. Transfer the breasts, skin side up, to a sheet pan fitted with a wire cooling rack. You can leave the breasts at this stage for 5 minutes or up to 1 hour.

Carefully pour the rendered duck fat out of each skillet into a heatproof container. You're going to want to keep that duck fat and use it to cook potatoes and other vegetables all winter long, so let it cool, seal it up, and tuck it in the fridge.

Just before you're ready to serve the duck, return about 1 tablespoon of duck fat to the largest of your large skillets and heat over medium-high. Place breasts skin side down in the hot skillet and cook just until the skin is re-warmed, golden brown, and crisp, 1 to 2 minutes. Flip, and cook until the meaty side is merely kissed with the hint of a brown crust, about 4 minutes. Transfer to a cutting board and let sit 10 minutes, then slice crosswise and fan the slices out on a serving platter. Sprinkle with flaky sea salt and freshly ground black pepper.

ESCAROLE SALAD WITH ORANGES, PISTACHIOS, AND PICKLED ONIONS

1 large or 2 small heads
    escarole

3 oranges, preferably all
    different colors (such as
    a navel, a Cara Cara, and
    a blood)

¼ cup (60 ml) freshly
    squeezed orange juice

¼ cup (60 ml) olive oil

2 teaspoons kosher salt

1 cup (55 g) Pickled Onions
    (page 44)

½ cup (65 g) roasted salted
    pistachios (shelled),
    coarsely chopped

SERVES 4 TO 6, RECIPE
EASILY DOUBLED TO SERVE
8 TO 12 OR HALVED TO
SERVE 2 TO 3

PREP THE ESCAROLE

Lay the head of the escarole on a cutting board like a bouquet of flowers, with the root base at one end. Slice the bouquet in half crosswise, then slice off the root base and discard. Separate the leaves, inspecting and discarding any leaves that are badly bruised, wilted, or browning. Wash, dry, and store your salad greens following instructions on page 53.

PREP THE ORANGES

Cut the nose and tail off an orange. On a cutting board, rest it on its flat base and use a small sharp knife to slice the peel off, starting at the top and tracing the contour of the orange down and around. Work your way around the circumference of the orange like this until no skin remains. Repeat with the remaining oranges, then slice into rounds. Pour any juices into a glass measuring cup, then squeeze enough orange juice to equal a total of ¼ cup (60 ml).

Whisk the olive oil and salt into the orange juice and set aside. (This is going to be your salad dressing!)

When ready to serve, transfer your prepped escarole to a very large bowl. Pour your salad dressing over, and use your hands to toss to coat. Add the orange slices, pickled onions, and half of the pistachios and toss to coat. Transfer to a serving platter or bowl (with your hands!) then sprinkle the remaining pistachios over the top and serve.

A VERY WINTERY BRAISED BEEF AND POLENTA DINNER

Here is a menu that leans into spending extra time at home and indoors in the winter with at least two days of mostly unattended slow cooking and roasting and braising to help keep you warm. And the food itself is here to warm you too: heavy, hearty, rich, meaty, cheesy . . . yum! My Italian friend Carola taught me how to make polenta concia like her family makes it, stirring chunks of Gorgonzola dolce and cubes of Fontina in at the end, and once you've had polenta like that there's really no going back. For a dinner party it's easier to make it in advance and bake it. I bury the cheese into the polenta in the baking dish while it's cool then bake, so that when you spoon into it to serve, little pockets of oozing melted cheese are revealed. Spoon red wine–braised beef ribs over the top and you just might start to wonder if you've died and gone to winter heaven.

Party Size
Serves 8 to 10, recipes easily halved to serve 4 to 5

Party Prep
Requires 1 to 2 days' advance prep; no real cooking before serving is required.

Sauce to Serve
Gremolata (page 47)

Optional Add-Ons
Bitter green salad dressed in Peppercorn Vinaigrette (page 51) or Lemony Vinaigrette (page 48)

Bread

Special Diets

PLANNING ADVICE

- Make the beef at least 1 and up to 2 days in advance.

- Make the stovetop part of the polenta at least 4 hours and up to 2 days in advance.

- The polenta has to bake in the oven for about 30 minutes before serving, so be sure to start heating your oven about 1 hour before you want to sit down to eat.

- Make the gremolata no more than 1 hour in advance so that it doesn't get wilty and weird.

For Other Dietary Restrictions

This menu is really not dairy-free friendly at all, so pick another menu if that's what you're working with. But if a dairy-free guest shows up unexpectedly, boil them some pasta to eat with their short ribs instead of the polenta.

To serve a vegetarian guest, simmer some white beans in tomato sauce with garlic and thyme until warm and fragrant, about 10 minutes, and that should do the trick to spoon over the polenta.

To serve a pescatarian guest, simmer some raw peeled and deveined shrimp in tomato sauce with garlic and thyme until the shrimp is opaque.

RED WINE–BRAISED SHORT RIBS

6 pounds (2.7 kg) beef
    short ribs
5 teaspoons kosher salt
1 tablespoon olive oil
2 onions, halved through the
    root (don't trim that root,
    it helps hold everything
    together)
2 whole heads garlic, cloves
    peeled and smashed
1 (4.4-ounce/130-g) tube
    double concentrated
    tomato paste
1 (750-ml) bottle red wine,
    something good enough
    to drink but not too fancy
4 sprigs fresh thyme
½ teaspoon crushed red
    pepper flakes

SERVES 8 TO 10, RECIPE
EASILY HALVED TO SERVE
4 TO 5

Heat the broiler to high.

Most braising recipes would have you individually sear each piece of meat, but I don't think that's worth the fuss, time, or stovetop spatter mess. Instead, I sear the whole batch at once in the broiler. Season the short ribs on all sides with salt, then arrange in a single layer on a sheet pan. Broil until the top side is deeply browned and crisped, 8 to 10 minutes, then flip and broil until the other side is also deeply browned and crisped, another 5 to 10 minutes. Set aside. Turn off the broiler and heat the oven to 300°F (150°C).

Meanwhile, in a large Dutch oven, heat the oil over medium-high until shimmering. Add the onion halves, cut side down, and garlic cloves and sear until lightly browned and fragrant, about 5 minutes. Add the tomato paste, stir to coat, then increase the heat to high and pour in the whole bottle of wine. Add the thyme and let simmer until the steam coming off the pot no longer smells super boozy, and the wine has reduced slightly, about 10 minutes. Add the short ribs (remove and discard any fat on the sheet pan), then cover with enough water to submerge the ribs (5 to 6 cups). Bring to a boil, then transfer to the oven and cook until the beef is super tender, about 2 hours. Let cool to room temperature, then chill the whole pot in the fridge or in a safe cold place (below 40°F [4.5°C] and above 32°F [0°C]) outside overnight. This overnight rest is essential to deepening the flavor and improving the texture of the meat.

An hour or two before serving, and definitely before your guests arrive because this can get a bit messy, remove the pot from its chilling spot and scrape the congealed fat off the top and discard. Gently warm the pot on the stove over medium-low heat just until the liquid is no longer congealed. Now it's time to sort the meat from the bones. Use a slotted spoon to scoop out all the pieces of meat and transfer to a large bowl or sheet pan. Pick out and discard the sprigs of thyme and onion halves, then simmer the remaining braising liquid over medium-high until thickened and reduced slightly, about 30 minutes. Meanwhile, once it's cool enough to touch, use your hands to pull the meat off the bones, and discard the bones and any cartilage. Be careful not to shred the meat too much—you want it to be in nice juicy chunks. Remove the pot of braising liquid from the stove and add the meat. Stir gently to combine and then let sit, covered, until just before serving. Re-warm over medium before transferring to a (preferably warm) serving platter with the braising liquid.

GORGONZOLA BAKED POLENTA

1 tablespoon kosher salt

2 cups (120 g) coarse polenta

1 cup (240 ml) whole milk

½ cup (1 ounce/50 g) finely
grated Parmesan cheese

1 teaspoon freshly ground
pepper

4 ounces (108 g) Gorgonzola
dolce, broken into ½-inch
(12-mm) pieces

4 ounces (108 g) Fontina
cheese, cut into ½-inch
(12-mm) cubes

SERVES 8 TO 10, RECIPE
EASILY HALVED TO SERVE
4 TO 5

In a large pot, bring 5 cups (1.2 L) water to a boil. Add the salt and polenta and whisk to combine. Lower the heat to the lowest setting and continue to cook, stirring often, until all the water has absorbed into the polenta and the polenta is very thick, about 10 minutes. Stir in the milk and cook, stirring often, until thick, another 10 minutes. Stir in the Parmesan and pepper. Transfer to a 1.5- to 2-quart (1.4- to 2-L) baking dish or gratin dish and smooth the top. Let cool until cool enough to stick a finger into, then scatter the Gorgonzola and Fontina pieces over the top, and press each into the center of the polenta with your fingers. Cover and chill for at least 4 hours and up to 2 days.

About 1 hour before you're ready to serve dinner, preheat the oven to 400°F (205°C).

Bake the polenta, uncovered, on the top rack of the oven until bubbling and golden brown, 20 to 30 minutes. Let sit 10 minutes before serving to avoid burning tongues.

A DINNER OF WARM CHEESY DUMPLINGS AND COLD CRUNCHY SALAD

If you've never made Marcella Hazan's tomato sauce with onions and butter, please do so for your next pasta night. It's magic. It's also the inspiration for the sauce in this menu, which I spice up with Calabrian chiles. (You might have to order them online, but they are very much worth it!) When I lived in Park Slope, I was around the corner from a lovely little Northern Italian restaurant called Al di Là, and I would go there often. Even though I'm gluten-free and couldn't eat them, their homemade pastas enchanted me, especially the malfatti, which they made with ricotta and swiss chard. I tried a few times to make gluten-free versions of it from scratch for myself, but eventually gave up in favor of spinach ricotta dumplings, which I promise work equally as well with all-purpose gluten-free flour as they do with regular wheat flour. They are a labor of love, but not actually difficult. And they make for a very cozy and impressive vegetarian dinner party. With that warm-cheesy-doughy-dumpling situation going on, I like a cold and crispy winter raw salad on my plate as well, featuring lots of spicy daikon and tart apples and plenty of fresh sweet basil.

Party Size
Serves 6, recipes easily
halved to serve 2 to 3

Party Prep
Advance prep is required,
but it can all be done in 1
day or split over 2 days.

Optional Add-Ons
Bread

A Simple Salad (page 53)

Special Diets

PLANNING ADVICE

- Forming and cooking the dumplings takes some concentration and can get a bit messy, so it's much less stressful if you do it before guests arrive—you can even do it the morning before a party. That's why I've built in the step of blasting the dumplings in a hot oven before serving (though that brown crisp edge is also a good reason for it).

- The tomato sauce for the dumplings can be made up to 5 days in advance, just rewarm it before serving.

> *For Other Dietary Restrictions*
>
> *This is one of those menus that really leans on dairy, and it's hard to make a dairy-free option that'll be as enticing. But if you do have a dairy-free guest show up unexpectedly, quickly boil them some pasta and serve it in a separate dairy-free marinara sauce.*

SPINACH AND RICOTTA DUMPLINGS IN SPICY TOMATO SAUCE

For the dumplings

3 (10-ounce/280-g)
   packages frozen spinach,
   defrosted and drained

1½ cups (370 g) whole milk
   ricotta

6 large eggs

¾ cup (70 g) finely grated
   Parmesan cheese, plus
   more for serving (84 g or
   3 ounces)

2 cloves garlic, finely grated

1 cup (128 g) all-purpose
   gluten-free or wheat flour

¼ teaspoon freshly grated
   nutmeg

1 teaspoon kosher salt, plus
   more for cooking

Olive oil, for sheet pan

For the sauce

1 (28-ounce/794-g) can
   whole peeled tomatoes

1 stick unsalted butter

1 onion, halved

2 teaspoons kosher salt

6 Calabrian chiles

SERVES 6, RECIPE EASILY
HALVED TO SERVE 2 TO 3

MAKE THE DUMPLINGS

Working in 3 batches, place the drained spinach in a clean dish towel and squeeze as hard as you can to get all the excess water out, then transfer to the bowl of a food processor. Pulse until finely chopped. Add the ricotta, eggs, Parmesan, garlic, flour, nutmeg, and salt to the spinach in the food processor and pulse to combine. Chill the mixture for at least 30 minutes and up to overnight.

Bring a large pot of salted water to a boil. To form the dumplings, use 2 soup spoons, one in each hand. Fill one spoon with a heaping spoonful of batter, then transfer the batter back and forth between both spoons, scraping it out of the full spoon with the empty one and pressing gently into the batter until a rough dumpling shape is formed. Use the empty spoon to scrape the dumpling out into the pot of boiling water.

Boil the dumplings in batches of about 12 until they float on the surface of the water and firm up slightly, 6 to 8 minutes per batch. Use a slotted spoon to transfer to an oil-greased sheet pan. Let cool to room temperature, then cover and chill for up to 2 days.

MAKE THE SAUCE

Use your hands to squeeze and crush the tomatoes into a large pot. Lower the tomatoes into the pot before you start squeezing if you want to avoid getting tomato guts on your chest. Add the butter, onion, salt, and chiles and heat over medium-high until simmering, then lower the heat and continue to simmer, stirring occasionally, until reduced and thickened, about 20 minutes. Remove from the heat and transfer to a blender. Puree until smooth. Transfer to a container and refrigerate for up to 5 days or transfer back to the pot to reheat and serve.

Preheat the oven to 500°F (260°C).

While the oven heats, heat the tomato sauce over medium-low until simmering, stirring occasionally.

Drizzle or brush the tops of the dumplings lightly with olive oil. Roast until lightly browned and warmed through, 8 to 10 minutes.

Spread the hot tomato sauce on a serving platter, then arrange the dumplings in a single layer on top. Sprinkle with Parmesan and serve.

CRUNCHY WINTER SALAD

1 large or 2 small daikon
   radishes, peeled and
   thinly sliced

2 fennel bulbs, thinly sliced

4 stalks celery, thinly sliced
   on a bias

2 green apples, thinly sliced

1 teaspoon kosher salt

2 tablespoons white
   balsamic or white wine
   vinegar

1 cup (40 g) loosely packed
   fresh basil leaves

SERVES 6, RECIPE EASILY
HALVED TO SERVE 2 TO 3

In a large bowl, place the thinly sliced radish, fennel, celery, and apples in a large bowl of ice water and let sit until ready to serve, up to 3 hours. This keeps everything safe from oxygen exposure, which would cause browning, but the ice also makes everything extra-crispy, so don't skip this step even if you're serving in 30 minutes. When ready to serve, drain and spin dry in a salad spinner if you have one, or spread out on a clean dish towel and pat dry. Transfer to a large salad or mixing bowl. Season with salt, and toss to combine. Then drizzle with the vinegar, and toss to combine again. Transfer to a serving platter and top with the basil to serve.

A STEAKHOUSE DINNER FOR A CROWD

It's steakhouse night, but you're staying home, and you can make everything almost entirely in advance. Searing individual steaks for each guest is just not a fun thing to do for a crowd, so instead I roast a whole New York strip roast. You've had a New York strip steak before, right? This is just a lot of strip steaks stuck together but reverse that because it hasn't been cut yet. Ask any butcher and they'll know exactly what you mean. I season it with only salt and pepper and cook it to medium-rare, exactly how I like my steak. Then each guest gets a slice topped with kelp butter, which is a fun way to season each steak with extra rich, salty-umami flavor. There's no creamed spinach or a separate potato side at my home steakhouse, but there is one big, gloriously creamy potato, kale, and butternut squash gratin, which can be made almost entirely a day in advance, and then rewarmed with cheese on top just before serving. You're going to need a lot of red wine to go with this menu.

Party Size	**Party Prep**	**Optional Add-Ons**
Serves 10 to 12	The menu can all be made in 1 day if necessary, but half the menu can be made up to 2 days in advance.	A Simple Salad (page 53)
		Special Diets

PLANNING ADVICE

- Make the kelp butter at least 6 hours and up to 1 week in advance.

- The roast takes about 2 hours to cook, but it can sit for up to 1 hour between roasting and searing, so start working on it at least 2 hours and up to 3 hours before your guests arrive.

- The gratin is a bit of a project, so make sure to leave plenty of time for yourself to make it. It can be made up to 1 day in advance.

For Other Dietary Restrictions

This menu is truly difficult to adapt for a vegan guest. If you know you've got a vegan friend coming, choose a different menu. If a vegan guest shows up unexpectedly, sauté some kale and garlic in olive oil in a skillet, add a drained can of white beans or chickpeas and a splash of vegetable broth, simmer until flavorful, season generously, and serve it over a big slice of toast with a drizzle of olive oil and apologize for the fact that they'll have to watch everyone else eat meat and dairy tonight.

If serving a vegetarian guest, the gratin is hearty enough to be their full meal, just be sure to add a salad. If serving a pescatarian guest, broil a cod fillet just until opaque, about five minutes, then melt kelp butter on top.

If serving a dairy-free guest, you can serve bread and salad to them and keep the butter on the side of the steak. But honestly this gratin is kind of cruel to serve in front of dairy-free guests: There's just so much dairy going on in it. So, if you have multiple dairy-free guests, make the Crispiest Roasted Potatoes and Artichokes (page 106) and Aioli (page 41) instead, and save the gratin for a time when everyone at the table can enjoy dairy together.

NEW YORK STRIP ROAST WITH BUTTER

For the kelp butter

½ cup (1 stick/55 g) best
    quality salted butter, at
    room temperature

1 tablespoon kelp flakes

For the roast

1 (5-pound/2.3-kg) boneless
    New York strip roast,
    untied

5 teaspoons kosher salt

5 teaspoons freshly ground
    black pepper

SERVES 10 TO 12

MAKE THE KELP BUTTER

In a medium bowl, place the softened butter and kelp flakes and go at it with a wooden spoon, stirring and mashing until the kelp is thoroughly incorporated into the butter. Transfer the butter mixture to a piece of parchment paper, patting it into a sort of log shape toward one long end of the parchment. Pull the parchment up and over the butter to secure the log, then roll it tightly into a uniform cylinder about 1½ inches (4 cm) wide, twisting the parchment around each end like an old-fashioned candy wrapper to secure. Chill until firm, at least 6 hours and up to 1 week.

MAKE THE ROAST

Pat the roast dry and season on all sides with the salt and pepper. Let sit 15 to 30 minutes while the oven heats to 350°F (175°C).

On a roasting pan, cook the the roast fat cap up until an instant-read thermometer inserted into the center of the roast registers 125°F (52°C) for medium-rare, 65 to 85 minutes. This is a good time to use one of those probe thermometers if you have one so you can watch the temperature from outside of the oven to pull it out at the exact right moment.

Remove from the oven and let stand for at least 15 minutes and up to 1 hour.

Before serving, heat the oven to broil. Broil the roast with the fat cap side facing up until crispy and re-warmed, 5 to 10 minutes. Slice and serve with the kelp butter. And don't worry, you don't have to let it rest again after reverse-searing; you already gave it a nice, good rest for the juices to redistribute.

BUTTERNUT SQUASH, POTATO, AND KALE GRATIN

2 tablespoons olive oil, plus
more for baking dish

2 bunches curly kale, torn
into small pieces

Kosher salt

3 cups (720 ml) heavy cream

3 cloves garlic, crushed

3 sprigs thyme

½ teaspoon freshly ground
nutmeg

Freshly ground black pepper

4 pounds (1.8 kg) russet
potatoes, peeled and very
thinly sliced

2 butternut squash necks
(2 pounds/910 g), peeled
and very thinly sliced

4 ounces (115 g) Gruyère,
finely grated

SERVES 10 TO 12

In a large deep skillet or pot, heat the oil, add the kale, and cook, stirring often, until fully wilted, about 3 minutes. Season with 1 teaspoon salt, and let cool.

In a medium pot, heat the cream, garlic, thyme, nutmeg, 1 teaspoon pepper, and 1 tablespoon salt just until boiling, then lower the heat and simmer for 10 minutes. Remove from the heat.

Heat the oven to 350°F (175°C).

Arrange the sliced potatoes, kale, and squash in a 4-quart (4-L) baking dish by making towers of the potatoes and squash in your hands, then laying each tower on its side in the baking dish and stuffing kale in between the cracks throughout. Pour the cream mixture over the vegetables. Cover tightly with foil and bake until tender, 60 to 70 minutes. Let cool. At this point, you can chill the gratin overnight.

Before serving, set the oven to broil. Top the gratin with the cheese and broil until bubbling and golden brown, 5 to 10 minutes.

A CREAM-FILLED WAY TO SERVE PORK AND MASH FOR DINNER

Continuing on my theme of leaving things simmering on the stove for as long and as often as I can in the winter, enter this braised pork shank. Pork shank is often overlooked, but it's a very good cut for braising, with lots of cartilage and connective tissue to enrich the broth. I use cross-cut shanks (just like osso buco steaks), sear them (under the broiler always—I don't believe in individually searing meat for braising), then simmer them in a simultaneously creamy and piquant concoction featuring wine, cream, mustard, broth, and punchy pickled green peppercorns. This cream and mustard braising method is very French, and my take on it was originally inspired by the mustard-braised rabbit served at the ever-charming French restaurant Buvette in New York City. All that sauce screams out to be poured over mashed potatoes. I add parsnips and a secret infusion of vanilla to my mashed potatoes here to give them a bit of alluring je ne sais quoi.

Party Size

Serves 4 to 6, recipes easily halved to serve 2 to 3 or doubled to serve 8 to 10

Party Prep

At least 1 day of advance prep is required.

Sauce to Serve (choose one!)

Pickled Shallot Salsa Verde (page 35)

Pickled Peppercorn Vinaigrette (page 51)

Optional Add-Ons

Greens simply dressed with Lemony Vinaigrette (page 48)

Bread

Special Diets

PLANNING ADVICE

- The pork is best made at least 1 day and up to 2 days before serving.

- The potatoes and parsnips can be boiled 1 day in advance, then make the mash up to 1 hour before serving.

- If making Pickled Shallot Salsa Verde, keep the pickled shallots separate from the herb oil mixture until just before serving so that the herbs don't brown.

> ### For Other Dietary Restrictions
>
> *To serve a vegetarian guest, sear some wild mushrooms in butter until golden-brown, then deglaze the skillet with a bit of white wine, whisk in a splash of heavy cream and a spoonful of Dijon, and simmer until thickened slightly. Season with salt and pepper and a pinch of capers or pickled peppercorns and serve instead of the pork.*
>
> *There is dairy in absolutely every part of this menu. So, if serving a dairy-free guest, choose a different menu please, rather than trying to modify.*

CREAM AND MUSTARD–BRAISED PORK SHANKS

6 pounds cross-cut pork
    shank steaks, each about
    2 inches (5 cm) thick
    (osso-bucco style)

1 tablespoon kosher salt, plus
    more to taste

1 tablespoon olive oil

6 shallots, finely chopped

2 cloves garlic, finely
    chopped

1½ cups (360 ml) white wine

4 sprigs thyme

2 bay leaves

¼ cup (57 g) smooth Dijon
    mustard

2 tablespoons whole-grain
    mustard

1 cup (240 ml) heavy cream

4 cups (960 ml) beef or
    chicken broth

1 tablespoon pickled green
    peppercorns or capers

SERVES 4 TO 6, RECIPE
EASILY HALVED TO SERVE
2 TO 3 OR DOUBLED TO
SERVE 8 TO 10

On a sheet pan, season the pork on all sides with salt and arrange in a single layer. Let sit while you heat your oven to broil.

Broil the pork, turning once halfway through, until deeply golden brown on all sides, 5 to 10 minutes. Set aside.

Meanwhile, in a Dutch oven or braising dish, heat the oil over medium-high. Add the shallots and garlic and cook, stirring often, until softened and translucent but not browned, 5 minutes. Pour in the white wine, thyme, and bay leaves and bring to a boil. Once boiling, add the broiler-seared pork shank pieces into the liquid, leaving behind and discarding any fat left in the pan.

In a small bowl or glass measuring cup, whisk together the Dijon, whole-grain mustard, and heavy cream, making sure you don't get any clumps of mustard, then pour the mixture into your pot along with the broth and peppercorns. Once the liquid in the pot is simmering, reduce the heat to low, partially cover the pot, and cook, stirring every once in a while, until the pork is so tender that it falls off the bone when gently prodded, about 3 hours. Cover, and let cool to room temperature, then chill the whole pot in the fridge or in a safe cold place (below 40°F [4.5°C] and above 32°F [0°C]) outside overnight.

An hour or two before serving, and before your guests arrive, remove the pot from its chilling spot, scrape the congealed fat off the top, and discard. Gently re-warm the pot on the stove just until the liquid is no longer congealed. Now it's time to sort the meat from the bones. Use a slotted spoon to scoop out all the pieces of meat and transfer to a large bowl or sheet pan. Pick out and discard the sprigs of thyme and bay leaves, and simmer the braising liquid over medium-high until thickened and reduced slightly, about 30 minutes. Meanwhile, once it's cool enough to touch, use your hands to pull the meat off the shank bones, then discard the bones and any cartilage. Set the meat aside. Once the braising liquid is a nice, thick, creamy sauce, turn off the heat and add the meat back into it. Stir to combine and then let sit, covered, until just before serving. Re-warm over medium before transferring to a (preferably warm) serving platter.

MASHED POTATOES AND PARSNIPS

4 pounds (1.8 kg) Yukon Gold potatoes, peeled and cut into 2- to 3-inch (5- to 7.5-cm) pieces

2 pounds (910 g) parsnips, peeled and cut into 1- to 2-inch (2.5- to 5-cm) pieces

Kosher salt

1 cup (240 ml) whole milk

½ cup (1 stick/115 g) unsalted butter, plus more for serving

2 cloves garlic

½ vanilla bean, seeds scraped, or ½ teaspoon vanilla extract

Freshly ground black pepper

SERVES 4 TO 6, RECIPE EASILY HALVED TO SERVE 2 TO 3 OR DOUBLED TO SERVE 8 TO 10

Place the potatoes and parsnips in a large pot and cover with cold water by at least 4 inches (10 cm). Salt generously. Bring to a boil over high heat, then lower to a simmer and continue to cook until the potatoes and parsnips are very tender when pierced with the tip of a knife but not to the point of falling apart, 20 to 25 minutes. Drain in a colander. At this point, you can chill the cooked potatoes and parsnips in an airtight container or bag overnight.

Meanwhile, in a small saucepan, heat the milk, butter, garlic, and vanilla over medium, just until boiling, then remove from the heat and let sit so the flavors infuse while the potatoes and parsnips cook.

For a fluffy, smooth mash, I like to use a ricer. Working in batches, squeeze the cooked parsnips and potatoes through the ricer back into the pot until you have a pot full of fluffy little white dots. Then add the milk mixture (discard the garlic cloves and vanilla bean first) and stir to combine with a wooden spoon until smooth. If the mixture is too thick, add a bit more milk. If you don't have a ricer, place the cooked potatoes and parsnips back in the pot and attack them with a potato masher. Once they're broken down a bit, add the milk mixture and keep mashing until smooth. You can keep the potatoes covered in their pot on the stove for up to 1 hour before serving. When ready to serve, give them a taste. Add more salt if needed (it's probably needed) and re-warm them over medium-high, stirring often and adding more milk if needed, until hot. Then swirl into a serving bowl or platter (preferably warm) and dot with butter and a grind of black pepper.

I'm not a religious person and don't believe in saying grace, per se, but I do believe it is useful to engage in an inclusive ritual to signify the beginning of a meal, especially a meal where I am intentionally gathering a group of people around a table for a special night. Everyday rituals to mark the beginning of a dinner are useful too, and can be anything from lighting a candle on the table before sitting down to holding hands and saying some kind of blessing of thanks. For example, a former boyfriend and I used to hold hands and kiss across the table before beginning to eat our dinner together, and I loved that ritual so much. Whatever it is, you want your ritual to imply: This is the beginning of a meal where we will pay attention to each other. We are gathering here together by choice, and we are going to be present in this moment at this table and be thankful for what we are about to eat and the company we share.

Whatever ritual I start a dinner party with, I like to do it at the moment when everyone has first found their seats. Kick off the meal, and *then* start passing platters around or getting up to serve yourselves from the buffet. This way, you aren't stuck staring down a plate full of food you want to start eating while everyone else is still serving themselves.

GIVE A TOAST

The easiest, and most familiar, way to mark the beginning of a special night: Raise your wine glass, say thank you all for being here, and clink glasses across the table with each guest, making sure not to cross arms (it's supposedly bad luck), and look each person in the eyes as your glasses touch. If the dinner is to mark a special occasion like a birthday or achievement or anniversary, toast to that. Toast to life. Toast to love. Toast to being able to safely gather together. Toast as many times as you want throughout the night as the spirit moves you.

A Toast for Each Guest

This is a ritual a learned from my Pops, who did it at his last milestone birthday dinner party: He stood up and toasted each guest at the table, who had all been carefully chosen for their importance in his life. He stood and talked for a long time, getting us all a bit drunk as we toasted each person in turn, but it was a beautiful ritual. No one loves a ritual more than me except my father. Each toast included how and why each guest was in his life, and why he valued his relationship to them. Tears were shed, laughter was contagious, and too much wine was sipped. It was an excellent dinner party. Next time you gather, no matter the occasion, try it out: Give a toast to each person at your table that night. Choose a theme to toast to: Share one accomplishment from each guest you are proud of, tell the story of how each guest came into your life, or choose something to thank each guest for.

HOLD HANDS

Some of your guests may giggle uncomfortably or crack jokes about being inducted into a cult when you ask everyone to hold hands around the table, but do not let that deter you. Once they are actually doing it, I promise they will appreciate it. Sit in silence for just a moment longer holding hands around the table and feel the presence of everyone connected by that touch. Feel the energy flowing from person to person and relish it. This is a truly special thing. Pass a squeeze around the table if you want, or simply say thank you. Take it a step further and continue holding hands while you say a blessing together. I know it might feel like *a lot* if this is new to you, but I believe we all crave this kind of human connection more than we're able to know or admit in our modern world, and I dare you to try it.

SAY A BLESSING

I grew up going to a Waldorf school, where a blessing before every meal was a part of our day. I still love the verse we said as blessing, and whenever my sisters or friends from Waldorf are with me at a table, we recite it together before dinner. It goes like this:

> *Earth, who gives to us this food,*
> *Sun, who makes it ripe and good,*
> *Dearest Earth and dearest Sun:*
> *We'll not forget what you have done.*
> *Blessings on our meal, and each other.*

Saying a blessing is a personal thing, and you should only say one that feels right to you and stands for what you believe in. If you can't find one that feels right, do like friends of mine did and write a blessing that represents exactly what you want to remember to be grateful for as you sit down to eat. If you are religious, find a blessing from your faith that feels right to you. But please, try not to alienate your guests with a blessing that is too specific or didactic.

READ A POEM

A favorite poem, or a poem that recently inspired you, or even a passage you recently read somewhere that's stuck with you can be a wonderful way to intentionally start a meal. Sometimes (especially when I host a gathering of all my dearest lady friends) I ask my guests to each bring a poem or passage that has inspired them recently to share with the table, and we take turns reading them throughout the meal instead of just one at the beginning. When in doubt, I always return to Mary Oliver and her poem "Wild Geese," which if you don't already know it, is worth looking up. It has soothed me on many occasions.

SING A SONG

For the musically inclined, kick your meal off by leading your guests in a song at the table. Better yet, a round. I'm a group singer but not a group song leader, so I leave this one to those who are.

SPRING

SPRING MENUS

After a long cozy winter, I'm always ready to rush into sweet, crunchy green things. More daylight and new life lead to lighter flavors and quicker-cooking things, but I still want plenty of warm things on the table. And so, my spring menus are a nice mix of warm and cold temperatures and cozy and fresh textures to fill this in-between season.

A FINGER-LICKING DINNER OF RIBS AND ASPARAGUS SALAD

Sticky, spicy ribs are always a fun party food. We should all gnaw on bones together more often. I discovered my love for lamb ribs by accident a couple years ago when pork spareribs weren't available, and now I prefer them. You may have to special order them from your butcher (or from D'Artagnan online) because they're not as common, but this recipe works equally well with pork. The glaze is a little bit agro-dolce and just spicy enough, and the charred vegetables and pickled onions are there to balance out all that rich, spicy sweetness.

Party Size	Sauce to Serve (choose one!)	Optional Add-Ons
Serves 4, recipes easily doubled to serve 8	Garlicky Yogurt Sauce (page 32)	Rice
		Flatbread
Party Prep	Tahini Sauce (page 42)	**Special Diets:**
Day-before or morning-of prep is required, plus about half an hour of before-serving prep.	Blender Spiced Green Sauce (page 43)	

PLANNING ADVICE

- The lamb ribs need to be slow-cooked for about 2 hours before they're ready to glaze, broil, and serve, but this can be done up to 2 days in advance, so plan accordingly.

- The pickled onions can be made up to 5 days in advance.

- Whichever sauce you choose, it can be made 1 day in advance and chilled.

- Broil the ribs before the vegetables, then pop the vegetables under the broiler while you slice and plate the ribs.

> ### For Other Dietary Restrictions
>
> *To accommodate a vegetarian or vegan guest, make them a hot honey cauliflower steak to eat instead of lamb ribs. Sear a cauliflower steak in olive oil until golden brown on both sides and fork-tender, then pour half measurements of all the glaze ingredients into the skillet with the cauliflower and cook for a few minutes until thickened, turning the cauliflower to coat.*

HOT HONEY LAMB RIBS

For the ribs

2 racks Denver lamb ribs
(about 2½ pounds/1.2 kg)
or 2 racks baby back pork
ribs

2 teaspoons kosher salt

2 teaspoons freshly ground
black pepper

1 teaspoon light brown sugar

For the glaze

¼ cup (60 ml) honey

¼ cup (60 ml) sherry or red
wine vinegar

2 tablespoons tamari or
gluten-free soy sauce

1 clove garlic, finely grated

1 tablespoon Aleppo-style
pepper flakes or ½
tablespoon crushed red
pepper flakes

SERVES 4, RECIPE EASILY
DOUBLED TO SERVE 8

MAKE THE RIBS

Preheat the oven to 325°F (165°C).

Score the fat cap on top of the ribs, cutting a cross-hatch pattern into it with a sharp knife but being careful not to cut all the way down to the bone. This will help all that fat render better. Place the ribs on a sheet pan and season on all sides with the salt, pepper, and brown sugar.

Add enough water to the sheet pan to go about a third up the sides, then cover tightly with foil and bake until the meat is fork-tender and the bones are starting to expose themselves, 1½ to 2 hours.

When the ribs are done cooking, remove from the oven. At this point you can let them cool completely, transfer to a storage container, and chill for up to 2 days. Or if serving soon, set them aside at room temperature for up to 1 hour. Discard that fatty cooking liquid.

MAKE THE GLAZE

In a small saucepan, heat the honey, vinegar, tamari, garlic, and chile flakes until boiling, reduce to a low simmer, and continue to cook just until the sauce coats the back of a spoon, about 8 minutes.

Let the ribs warm to room temperature if chilled, then brush all sides with half of the glaze and arrange meaty side up on a foil-lined sheet pan. Heat your broiler to high. Broil until the ribs are lightly charred and warmed through, 1 to 3 minutes. Brush the remaining glaze over the top and transfer to a cutting board. Slice into individual ribs and transfer to a serving platter.

CHARRED ASPARAGUS AND FENNEL

2 bunches thin asparagus,
   stems trimmed
1 large or 2 small bulbs
   fennel, cut into ¼-inch
   (6-mm) slices
¼ cup (60 ml) olive oil, plus
   more for drizzling
1 teaspoon kosher salt
½ teaspoon freshly ground
   black pepper
1 cup (30 g) parsley leaves
½ cup Pickled Onions
   (page 44)
Flaky sea salt, for serving

SERVES 4, RECIPE EASILY
DOUBLED TO SERVE 8

Preheat the oven to broil.

On a sheet pan, toss the asparagus and fennel in the oil, salt, and pepper. Broil until lightly charred, 4 to 6 minutes. Transfer to a serving platter and toss with the parsley and onions. Drizzle with olive oil and sprinkle with flaky salt.

A SPRING CHICKEN AND SALAD DINNER

Roast chicken and a salad will always be one of my favorite dinners. It's the perfect mix of cozy and fresh, warm and cold. It feels especially appropriate in the spring, when that salad can be abundantly crunchy and fresh with baby lettuce. I once had a tahini-dressed salad at Sofreh (my favorite Persian restaurant in Brooklyn) with slivers of dates in it, and I've been trying to re-create that salad ever since, including here in this menu. To give the date slices a crunchy exterior, I fry them in a bit of oil first. I like to roast a chicken in halves rather than whole, because it cooks faster and more evenly, you get more crispy skin, and it's easier to scale it up for a crowd. A buttermilk brine is, of course, a very well-known way to get chicken juicier and more tender before frying or roasting, but I never have buttermilk in my fridge (I know, I know) so yogurt is what I turn to instead; I like the extra bit of tartness it lends.

Party Size	Sauce to Serve	Optional Add-Ons
Serves 6 to 8, recipes easily halved to serve 3 to 4	(choose one or both)	Simple steamed potatoes or rice
	Tahini Sauce (page 42)	
Party Prep	Blender Spiced Green Sauce (page 43)	Bread
At least 1 day of advance prep is required.		**Special Diets**

PLANNING ADVICE

- The chicken needs to brine overnight (or up to 2 days).

- Start roasting your chicken 1 hour before you want to sit down to eat to accommodate for roasting and resting time.

- The radishes can be sliced and chilled up to 1 day in advance.

- Prep your greens and salad dressing before your guests arrive if you can, but if you can't, put your guests to work helping you with these tasks.

- Both sauces can be made up to 1 day in advance.

> *For Other Dietary Restrictions*
>
> *To serve a vegan or vegetarian guest, roast a small tray of spring vegetables (asparagus or small young carrots perhaps) and canned chickpeas tossed in a bit of olive oil, salt, and pepper in a 400°F (205°C) oven until lightly browned for them to eat with the sauce and salad instead of the chicken.*

YOGURT-BRINED CHICKEN HALVES

2 cups (480 ml) plain full-fat
yogurt

3 tablespoons kosher salt

4 chicken halves (or 2
chickens, backbones
removed, cut in half
through the breastbone)

SERVES 6 TO 8, RECIPE
EASILY HALVED TO
SERVE 3 TO 4

In a medium bowl, whisk together the yogurt, salt, and 1 cup (240 ml) water. Place the chicken halves in a large resealable gallon bag and pour the yogurt mixture over. Seal, pressing out all the air, and toss to coat the chicken halves well. Chill overnight or up to 2 days.

When ready to roast, remove the chicken from the fridge and let warm slightly while you heat the oven to 400°F (205°C). Remove the chicken halves from the bag, shake off any excess yogurt, and arrange, skin side up, in a single layer on a sheet pan.

Roast in the top third of the oven, rotating the pan once halfway through cooking, until the chicken skin is golden brown and crisp and an instant-read thermometer inserted in the thickest part of the breast registers 155°F (69°C), 35 to 45 minutes. (The temperature will climb to 165°F [74°C] as the chicken rests). Let the chicken halves rest on the pan at least 15 minutes and up to 30 minutes. Serve on a cutting board with a sharp knife, or cut into quarters and transfer to a serving platter.

SPRING GREENS WITH FRIED DATES

4 small heads lettuce, such
    as little gem, baby Bibb,
    or baby romaine
6 radishes, thinly sliced
3 tablespoons olive oil,
    divided
8 Medjool dates, pitted
    and sliced into quarters
    lengthwise
2 tablespoons Tahini Sauce
    (page 42)
2 tablespoons lemon juice
Kosher salt and freshly
    ground black pepper
Fresh chives and/or fresh dill,
    for topping

SERVES 6 TO 8, RECIPE
EASILY HALVED TO SERVE
3 TO 4

Slice the root base off each head of lettuce, then separate the leaves, inspecting and discarding any leaves that are badly bruised, wilted, or browning. Wash, dry, and store according to the directions on page 53.

Place your thinly sliced radishes in a resealable container, top with ice and water, and refrigerate for up to 1 day. This trick not only lets you prep your radishes in advance, but it also makes them extra crispy, which is a very good thing. If not prepping in advance, do this anyway—just let them sit for at least 10 minutes to get that ice water crunch. When ready to assemble the salad, drain the radishes well in a colander, shaking off as much excess water as possible.

Just before serving, in a large cast-iron or nonstick skillet over medium-high, heat 1 tablespoon of the oil. Add the date strips, toss to coat, and cook, tossing occasionally, until the dates are crisped and darkened in color, about 3 minutes. Transfer to a plate.

Transfer the lettuce and radishes to a large bowl and season with 1 teaspoon kosher salt. Toss gently with your hands to combine.

Whisk together the remaining 2 tablespoons of olive oil, the tahini sauce, and lemon juice, then drizzle over the salad and toss gently with your hands to coat. Taste a dressed leaf and add more salt if needed. Transfer to a serving platter (still with your hands to avoid bruising the delicate leaves) and top with the fried dates, chives and/or dill, and freshly ground black pepper.

A QUICHE AND LEEKS DINNER YOU MIGHT WANT FOR BRUNCH

Depending on your needs and the weather, this menu can be served completely cold, or warm. Polenta molded into a springform pan is my ideal gluten-free crust for a quiche. I love how it gets crispy on the top edges and folds over this custardy quiche like a cozy nest. I keep the flavor of my quiche pure—simple eggs and cream, almost like a savory cheesecake—which is nicely balanced by a sweet-tart, classic French leeks vinaigrette. I will forgive you if you serve this menu for brunch (it'd make a great brunch), but I like it for dinner.

Party Size

Serves 6 to 8

Party Prep

The whole menu can be made in 1 day, but it's easier to split the prep up over 2 days, since the quiche can be made in advance.

Sauce to Serve

Aioli (page 41)

Optional Add-Ons

Bread

A Simple Salad (page 53)

Special Diets

PLANNING ADVICE

- The polenta needs to be made 1 day (or at least 2 hours) before you can make the quiche, so plan accordingly. The quiche can be made a day before, or anytime up to 2 hours before, serving.

- The leeks can be made a few hours before serving and they can sit out at room temperature until ready to serve.

- The aioli can be made 1 day in advance and chilled. If it solidifies in the fridge, just whisk in a bit of water before serving to loosen it.

> ### For Other Dietary Restrictions
>
> *If you need a vegan or dairy-free menu, this quiche is really not the thing. But if a vegan or dairy-free guest shows up unexpectedly, sauté some kale or fresh green vegetables (whatever you have on hand) in some olive oil and garlic, add some rinsed canned beans, and sauté until warmed through. Season liberally and serve with toast and extra olive oil in place of the quiche. The leeks are vegan-friendly, but remember that aioli is not!*

POLENTA-CRUSTED DEEP-DISH QUICHE

For the polenta

1 teaspoon kosher salt

1 cup (120 g) polenta (coarse cornmeal)

½ cup (1 ounce/50 g) finely grated Parmesan cheese

1 teaspoon freshly ground black pepper

2 tablespoons butter, plus more for pan

For the filling

8 large eggs

1 cup (240 ml) heavy cream

1 cup (240 ml) sour cream

½ cup (120 ml) whole milk

2 tablespoons smooth Dijon mustard

1½ teaspoons kosher salt

SERVES 6 TO 8

MAKE THE POLENTA

In a medium pot, bring 3 cups (720 ml) water to a boil over high. Add the salt and reduce the heat to medium-low. Stirring constantly with a wooden spoon, gradually stream in the polenta. Cook, stirring often, until thick and creamy, 10 to 15 minutes. Remove from the heat and stir in the Parmesan, pepper, and butter. Let cool to room temperature. Generously butter the bottom and sides of a 9-inch (23-cm) springform pan. Scoop the polenta into the pan and use your hands to press it evenly into the bottom and up the sides to form your quiche crust. It's supposed to be a thick, rustic crust, so don't worry about getting it too thin or perfect anywhere. Cover and refrigerate at least 2 hours or overnight.

MAKE THE FILLING

Preheat the oven to 325°F (165°C).

In a large bowl, whisk together the eggs, heavy cream, sour cream, milk, mustard, and salt until smooth. Transfer to the chilled pan of polenta crust, set it on a sheet pan in case it spills or leaks during baking, and bake in the center of the oven until the egg filling is set, 70 to 80 minutes. Let cool at least 20 minutes or all the way to room temperature before serving. Once it cools to room temperature, you can cover it and refrigerate for up to 1 day before serving. Let it come to room temperature before serving. When ready to serve, release the springform and, with the help of a wide spatula and maybe even a friend, carefully transfer to a serving platter or cutting board. Cut into wedges to serve.

LEEKS VINAIGRETTE

10 to 12 medium leeks

¼ cup (60 ml) olive oil

¼ cup (60 ml) sherry or red wine vinegar

1 small shallot, finely chopped

1 tablespoon fresh thyme leaves

1 teaspoon Dijon mustard

1 teaspoon honey

1 teaspoon kosher salt

1 teaspoon freshly ground black pepper

SERVES 6 TO 8, EASILY
HALVED TO SERVE 3 TO 4

Set a steamer insert into a large pot filled with about 2 inches (5 cm) of water, cover, and bring to a boil over high heat.

Meanwhile, prep the leeks. Cut the hairy root base off the end of each leek, then cut off the dark green parts and discard both. Slice the white and light green parts into 3- to 4-inch (7.5- to 10-cm) pieces, and place in a colander. Wash well, then transfer to the steamer insert, cover, and steam on high heat until you can easily slide a paring knife through a leek, about 15 minutes.

While the leeks steam, make the dressing. In a small bowl, whisk together the olive oil, vinegar, shallot, thyme, mustard, honey, salt, and pepper, then set aside.

Transfer the leeks to a serving platter, re-whisk the dressing to re-emulsify it, and pour it over the leeks. Turn the leeks to coat and let sit for at least 10 minutes and up to 2 hours. Before serving, spoon some of the dressing from the platter over the top and finish with a grind of some fresh ground pepper.

A MAKE-AHEAD PORK TACO DINNER

This taco party menu works in any season of the year, and it is an excellent reason to keep a slow cooker around. Slow cookers and pork get along so well. (You'll see I pull this trick often; pork shows up in a slow cooker again in Summer, page 200.) This is not a traditional carnitas recipe, but traditional Mexican carnitas is often cooked with orange juice to help tenderize and flavor the meat, and I borrow that technique here by throwing the whole orange rind in the slow cooker with the pork to infuse it with extra orange flavor as it cooks. Rather than a slaw with small shreds of cabbage that fall out of a taco all over your plate, I like to make slaw with large pieces of cabbage leaf softened by scrunching and massaging. And if you want to eat it as a salad on the side instead of tucking it into your tacos, it works equally well.

Party size

Serves 8 to 10

Party Prep

At least 2 days of advance prep are required, and the menu can be prepared almost entirely in advance.

Sauce to Serve

Creamy Jalapeño Sauce
(page 38)

Optional Add-Ons

Sliced avocado

Sour cream

Pickled Onions (page 44)

Special Diets

PLANNING ADVICE

- The pork is best started 3 days in advance. On the first day, marinate it. On the second day, cook it. On the day of the party, shred and reheat it.

- To warm the tortillas, it's best to sear them one by one on a very hot cast-iron skillet until they char and slightly puff, flipping once halfway through. Wrap the tortillas in a dish cloth and place in a bowl to keep warm at the table. This is a great task to assign to a helpful guest. If you don't have extra hands or time, wrap all your tortillas in a dish cloth followed by foil, and then pop them in a hot oven until warmed through.

- The pickled onions can be made up to 5 days in advance.

- The creamy jalapeño sauce is best made the same day it's served, but you can make it a few hours in advance.

For Other Dietary Restrictions

To serve a vegetarian or vegan guest, mash and fry some cooked pinto beans in olive oil over medium-high heat for 5 to 10 minutes until the texture of lumpy mashed potatoes to make refried beans (or just buy some in a can and heat them!) to serve in place of the pork.

If serving a dairy-free guest, don't add sour cream.

CITRUS-CHILE SLOW-COOKED PORK

2 tablespoons kosher salt

1 tablespoon brown sugar

1 tablespoon chili powder,
preferably chipotle

1 (6-pound/2.7-kg) skinless,
boneless pork shoulder
roast, untied

2 navel oranges, halved

1 large onion, peeled and
halved

4 cloves garlic, lightly
crushed

2 cinnamon sticks

Tortillas, for serving

SERVES 8 TO 10

In a small bowl, mix the salt, sugar, and chili powder. Rub all over the pork, and let sit at room temperature for about 30 minutes or cover and chill overnight.

Transfer the pork to a 6-quart (5.7-L) or larger slow cooker insert. Squeeze the juice from the oranges over the pork, then put the oranges in there, too. Add the onion, garlic, and cinnamon sticks. Cook on high for 6 hours or low for 8 hours until the pork is super-duper tender and falling apart.

Using tongs, transfer the pork to a sheet pan and let cool slightly. Strain the juices left behind in the slow cooker through a fine-mesh sieve into a large heatproof measuring cup or bowl. Let sit 10 minutes, then spoon off and discard the fat. Using two forks or tongs, shred the pork into bite-size pieces, discarding any large pieces of fat that you find in the process. Transfer back to the slow cooker insert along with the degreased juices. If serving within the hour, keep heated using the warm setting of your slow cooker. If serving in a day or two, tuck the slow cooker insert in the fridge or hide in a cold garage or covered porch (below 40°F [4.5°C] and above 32°F [0°C]), or transfer to a food storage container and store in the fridge. When ready to serve, re-warm in the slow cooker on low or in a large pot over low heat.

TO ROAST IN THE OVEN

Place the seasoned pork in a large Dutch oven, cover, and roast in 350°F (175°C) oven, basting occasionally, until the meat super tender and falling apart, 6 to 7 hours.

SCRUNCHED CABBAGE SLAW

1 large or 2 small green
    cabbages (2 pounds/910 g)

1 tablespoon kosher salt, plus
    more to taste

3 tablespoons rice or apple
    cider vinegar

2 teaspoons brown sugar

2 small serrano chiles, thinly
    sliced

1 cup (30 g) cilantro leaves
    and tender stems

1 cup (65 g) roasted salted
    pumpkin seeds (pepitas)

SERVES 8 TO 10, EASILY
HALVED TO SERVE 4 TO 5

Cut the cabbage into quarters, cut out and discard the stem, and separate the leaves into a large bowl. Toss with the salt and use your hands to scrunch, squeeze, and massage the cabbage. Let sit about 10 minutes to allow the salt to work its way into the cabbage to help soften it further. Add the vinegar and sugar and toss to coat well. Let sit another 10 minutes or up to 1 hour. Before serving, toss in the serrano, cilantro, and pumpkin seeds, then transfer to a serving platter, leaving any juices that accumulate in the bowl behind.

A BUNCH OF SPRING THINGS TO DIP IN AIOLI FOR DINNER

This is a dinner to celebrate all the bright crunchy green things of spring! It can be eaten exclusively with your hands and prepped entirely in advance. You can pack it up and take it on a picnic, serve it on your lawn, or sit around the dining room table casually grazing arms with the person next to you as you reach across for another shrimp. I like to boil shrimp with the shells on because it's less work for me. It also keeps the shrimp more tender, juicy, and flavorful, and it creates a fun ice-breaking project for guests to peel shrimp themselves and get a little dirty as they eat. Set out a few empty bowls around the table for people to dump shrimp shells in and save them to make a shrimp stock!

Party Size
Serves 8, recipes easily halved to serve 4 or quartered to serve 2

Party Prep
Everything can be made up to a day in advance, or within an hour or two of serving.

Sauce to Serve
Aioli (You'll want to double it if serving 8—page 41)

Optional Add-Ons
French bread

Green salad, simply dressed with Lemony Vinaigrette (page 48)

Special Diets

PLANNING ADVICE

- The aioli can be made 1 day in advance and chilled. If it solidifies in the fridge, just whisk in a bit of water before serving to loosen it.

- Everything for this menu can be cooked and sliced the day before serving, so all you have to do is assemble platters to serve.

For Other Dietary Restrictions

To serve a vegetarian guest, make sure you add bread and salad and they'll be fine skipping the shrimp.

To serve a vegan guest, buy some vegan mayonnaise, stir some freshly grated garlic into it, and serve that to them to dip their spring things into, along with the bread and salad.

PEEL & EAT BOILED SHRIMP

2 pounds (910 g) jumbo
(16 to 20 per pound)
shell-on shrimp

2 lemons, halved, plus more
for serving

½ cup (66 g) kosher salt

2 tablespoons white sugar

2 bay leaves

SERVES 8, RECIPE EASILY
HALVED TO SERVE 4 OR
QUARTERED TO SERVE 2

Ask your fishmonger to give you deveined and "easy-peel" shell-on shrimp if you can. If you can't, prep them yourself. Here's how: Using scissors, snip down through the center of the curved back of each shell from the top to the base of the tail. You want to snip through both the shell and the very top layer of flesh, exposing the digestive tract of the shrimp. If you look at the severed head top, there's a natural hole; start snipping from there and the digestive tract will be easily revealed. Then, using a paring knife, tease out and discard the vein that runs down the center. If this process makes you squeamish, wear gloves! You'll get the hang of it quickly and find that it's much easier than peeling raw shrimp.

Fill a large pot with 12 cups (3 L) water, then squeeze in the juice from the lemons and add the squeezed halves to the pot for extra lemon infusion. Stir in the salt, sugar, and bay leaves and heat over high until boiling.

Set a large bowl of ice water next to the stove to use to stop the shrimp from over-cooking.

Add the prepared shrimp to the boiling water and cook, stirring often, just until all the shrimp are pink and opaque, about 3 minutes. Using a slotted spoon, immediately transfer the shrimp to the waiting ice bath and let sit until cooled. Then drain and pat dry with a clean towel. Chill in a resealable container or bag for up to 1 day, until ready to serve. Serve with lemon wedges alongside.

SPRING THINGS GRAND AIOLI

2 pounds (910 g) baby new
potatoes

1 bunch asparagus, trimmed

1 pound (455 g) sugar snap
peas, strings removed

3 romaine hearts or heads
of little gem lettuce,
quartered

1 bunch breakfast radishes,
halved

4 mini seedless cucumbers,
quartered lengthwise

Lemon wedges and flaky
salt, for serving

Aioli, for dipping (page 41)

SERVES 8, RECIPE EASILY
HALVED TO SERVE 4 OR
QUARTERED TO SERVE 2

In a large pot of generously salted water, place the potatoes and bring to a boil over medium-high heat. Cook until the potatoes are fork-tender, 10 to 15 minutes. Use a slotted spoon or spider to transfer the potatoes to a large bowl of ice water and chill until cold, about 3 minutes, but leave that pot boiling on the stove.

Add the asparagus and snap peas to the pot of boiling water and boil until fork-tender and bright green, about 3 minutes. Meanwhile, remove the potatoes from the ice water. Spread them out on a clean dish towel to dry. Use a slotted spoon or spider to transfer the asparagus and snap peas to the ice water and soak just until cooled, then drain and spread out with the potatoes. Let sit covered in a damp towel at room temperature for up to 1 hour before serving, or chill for up to 1 day in an airtight container.

To serve, arrange sections of the potatoes, asparagus, snap peas, lettuce wedges, radishes, and cucumbers on a serving platter. If everything doesn't fit on one platter, keep the potatoes separate in their own bowl and all the colorful things together on one platter. Drizzle with lemon juice and sprinkle with flaky salt. Serve with aioli for dipping.

A WHOLE SIDE OF SALMON AND CELERY FRUIT SALAD FOR DINNER

This menu is for the end of spring when it's kind of almost summer and apricots and cherries are popping up in all the markets. Or serve it in early summer and keep serving it until stone fruit season runs out, each time with a different fruit. Apricots are my favorite to pair with celery, but they all get along quite well and play a crunchy-sweet supporting role to a majestic whole side of buttery salmon. I like to serve my salmon at room temperature, roasted in a low oven just to the point of doneness.

Party Size
Serves 8 to 10

Party Prep
No advance prep required; the whole menu can be prepped and served within an hour or so.

Sauce to Serve
(choose one!)

Garlicky Yogurt Sauce
(page 32)

Aioli (page 41)

Optional Add-Ons
Bread

Special Diets

PLANNING ADVICE

- Whichever sauce you choose, it can be made 1 day in advance and chilled. If the aioli solidifies in the fridge, just whisk in a bit of water before serving to loosen it.

- If you don't get all your salad ingredients chopped before your guests arrive, set them to work chopping—it's a good group activity.

- The salmon can be roasted 1 day in advance, but it is best made the day of the party and can be roasted up to 1 hour before serving.

For Other Dietary Restrictions

To serve a vegetarian guest, you can roast a block of feta for them to enjoy with the salad, and make sure to add bread to the menu.

For a vegan guest, make Skillet Socca (page 28) and Blender Spiced Green Sauce (page 43) for them to enjoy with the salad.

For a dairy-free guest, make sure not to serve yogurt sauce.

SLOW-ROASTED SIDE OF SALMON

1 (3½- to 4-pound/1.6- to 1.8-kg) whole side of salmon or steelhead trout, skin on

¼ cup (60 ml) olive oil, plus more for serving

4 teaspoons kosher salt

2 teaspoons freshly ground black pepper

3 lemons, cut into wedges, for serving

Flaky sea salt, for serving

SERVES 8 TO 10

Preheat the oven to 300°F (150°C).

Place the salmon on a sheet pan and pour the olive oil over it, then turn the salmon to completely coat in the oil. Season both sides with the salt and pepper, landing skin side down on a sheet pan. Roast until the fish is opaque throughout and just able to easily flake when pressed, 20 to 30 minutes. Be careful not to overcook—the time it takes will depend on the thickness of your side of salmon, so start checking after 20 minutes. Let cool to room temperature. The salmon can sit at room temperature, loosely covered with parchment, for up to 1 hour. If you need to make it in advance, cover it well once cool and chill overnight. Let come to room temperature from the fridge for 45 minutes to 1 hour before serving.

Here's the trick to leave the skin behind without actually having to skin the fish: Slide two spatulas between the skin on the sheet pan and the cooked fish, working from opposite sides at the same time, then carefully lift the fish and transfer it to a serving platter. Best to have that serving platter right next to your sheet pan. If the fish breaks while you transfer, don't sweat it—it's going to get flaked into pieces as people serve themselves anyway. Drizzle with olive oil and lemon juice and sprinkle with flaky salt, then serve with the lemon wedges alongside.

CELERY AND STONE FRUIT SALAD

2 bunches celery, stalks
    separated and thinly
    sliced on a diagonal,
    leaves reserved

2 teaspoons kosher salt,
    divided

¼ cup (60 ml) olive oil

¼ cup (60 ml) white wine
    vinegar

1 teaspoon honey

2 teaspoons freshly ground
    black pepper

6 apricots or four peaches,
    sliced, or 8 ounces (227 g)
    cherries, pitted and
    halved

1 cup (30 g) mint leaves

1 cup (95 g) sliced almonds,
    lightly toasted

SERVES 8 TO 10, EASILY
HALVED TO SERVE 4 TO 5

Toss the celery in a large bowl with 1 teaspoon of the salt, then let sit for at least 10 minutes and up to 1 hour.

In a small bowl or measuring cup, whisk together the oil, vinegar, honey, remaining teaspoon of salt, and pepper.

Add the celery leaves, stone fruit, mint leaves, and almonds to the bowl of celery, pour the dressing over, and toss gently with your hands to combine. Use your hands to lift the salad out of the bowl and onto a serving platter, leaving any remaining dressing in the bowl behind.

QUESTIONS FOR THE TABLE

There's always a moment at a dinner party when conversation pauses. It usually happens ten to fifteen minutes after everyone has served themselves (though I've never actually timed it)—the pleasantries and small talk exchanged with the person next to you have passed, the exclamations over food have died out, a toast or two have been given, and people are just eating. This is the moment when, if the mood feels right, I like to ask a question for the table. It ties the group together into one conversation, and it lets everyone peacefully chew their food and listen while one person at a time speaks. It's a great ice breaker for guests who don't know each other, and a fun way to make sure each person at the table has a chance to speak, no matter how naturally outgoing they are. But it's not just for people who've never met—it can center and focus a conversation among old friends or family—and it is the easiest solution to move the banter away from gossip, politics, or the weather as needed.

Sometimes I make up a question on the spot as the spirit moves me, but more often than not I've thought about it earlier in the day and have a few in mind to choose from. I've been playing this game so long that I now have to remember which questions I've asked which guests. I once asked a question I'd posed to the same group a year before—but don't worry, my friends didn't let me get away with that, and neither will yours. Below are lots of questions I've used before as well as a few I still want to try. I've divided them into three categories for you, which I hope will help inspire more questions of your own. You may recognize that some of these questions are borrowed from and/or inspired by the classic Proust Questionnaire, and some are borrowed from and/or inspired by The 36 Questions That Lead to Love and yes, I also have used these questions on first dates before, as should you. The goal of all these questions is to get each person to tell a story about themselves, and to help your guests get better acquainted with each other.

FOR A LAUGH

Questions for when you want to lift the mood and inspire stories that should make everyone laugh.

- What's your most embarrassing travel story?

- Did you ever get sent to the principal's office in elementary school? What for?

- What was your best Halloween costume ever?

- Tell us about your first kiss.

- When was the first time you got drunk? What happened?

- Did you ever sneak out of the house when you were in high school? How did you do it? Where did you go?

- Describe the (imaginary) restaurant of your dreams. What does it serve? What is the interior like? Where is it?

- What's the best party you've ever been to? Tell us about it.

FOR DEEPER MEANING

These are questions for digging a little deeper into the personal—safer for old friends or if you just want to dive right into the possibility of tears being shed. (I come from a family who openly cry at the dinner table from time to time, so I'm all about diving in.)

- What are you most thankful for at this very moment?

- What is something you've found easier to forgive or understand as you got older?

- What are you the most afraid of? Why?

- Tell us about a challenge you are proud of overcoming.

- What's inspiring you right now?

- What do you think is the most important trait to have in a friendship?

- What is something that happened to you that seemed really bad at the time, but ultimately proved to change your life for the better?

- Knowing what you know now, if you could offer your twenty-year-old self (vary this age based on guests' age, of course!) one piece of advice from Current You, what would it be?

TO SPARK DEBATE

Questions that are open to debate, and may take a little longer for people to decide how to respond to, can fuel some passionate conversation.

- You've got a crystal ball that can tell you any one thing you want to know about the future. What's your question? Why?

- You're going into a bunker for the foreseeable future. That bunker is full of all the bare necessities of survival. You can bring only one object with you for your comfort and enjoyment: What would that object be? Why?

- Your home is on fire and all pets and humans are safe. You can grab one object from your home to save from the fire: What would it be? Why?

- If you could have any superpower, what would it be? Why?

- If you were to die and come back as an animal, what animal would it be? Why?

- Do you think it's ever okay to lie? If so, when? (Also: When was the last time you lied?)

- Would you rather forego all sauces and condiments or all desserts for the rest of your life?

SUMMER

SUMMER MENUS

There's an ease and fun to summer dinner parties. They tend to start and end later. They're often eaten outside, sometimes even on vacation. When summer produce explodes, my cooking gets even simpler. A ripe tomato needs no help from me to taste good, so I slice it and sprinkle it with salt and serve. Many of these menus are served cold or at room temperature because it's easier and because it's just too hot to be cooking while entertaining. And with that in mind, with one small exception, I never ask you to turn on the stovetop in these menus. If we're cooking, we're grilling or doing it far in advance in the oven or slow cooker.

A Cold Lamb Roast and Tomato Salad Dinner

COLD ROSEMARY-ROASTED LAMB
LOIN 188

•

MARINATED WHITE BEAN AND
TOMATO SALAD 190

A Dinner of Grilled Chicken and Peppers

GRILLED PAPRIKA CHICKEN WITH
GARLIC VINEGAR 194

•

CHARRED AND MARINATED SWEET
AND SHISHITO PEPPERS 196

A Mustard Pork Roast and Wedge Salad Dinner

SLOW-COOKER PORK ROAST 200

•

LITTLE GEM CAESAR WEDGES 202

A Quick Way to Serve Grilled Steak and Melon Salad for Dinner

LEMONGRASS-GINGER COCONUT
GRILLED STEAK 206

•

MELON, CUCUMBER, AND
AVOCADO SALAD 208

A Vacation-Ready Grilled Fish and Corn Boil Dinner

GRILLED SWORDFISH STEAKS 212

•

ONE-POT POTATOES, GREEN
BEANS, AND CORN WITH
MISO-PEPPER BUTTER 214

A Very Summery Grilled Veggies and Tomato Salad Dinner

ZA'ATAR GRILLED EGGPLANT
AND ZUCCHINI 218

•

BLUE CHEESE, TOMATO, AND
HERB SALAD 220

A COLD LAMB ROAST AND TOMATO SALAD DINNER

You may need to make a trip to your local butcher or place a special order at your grocery store for it, but a boneless lamb loin roast is so worth that very small hassle. Smaller, more tender, and quicker-cooking than a boneless leg of lamb roast, it's my favorite way to serve lamb to a crowd in the summer. Because it's so tender, it's really good served cold, thinly sliced with a fun sauce drizzled on top. A big hunk of roast red meat on the hottest night of the summer sounds terrible to me, but a slice of cold lamb loin doused in a zesty green sauce full of bites of pickled shallot is shockingly refreshing. And best of all, it can be roasted up to 2 days in advance, then simply sliced just before serving, so reasons for breaking into a sweat while hosting are slightly diminished. And since I'm trying not to sweat, I keep the rest of the menu as make-ahead friendly as possible, too.

Party Size

Serves 4 to 6, recipes easily doubled to serve 8 to 10

Party Prep

Everything can be prepared entirely in advance; you need to start at least 1 day ahead.

Sauces to Serve (choose one or two)

Pickled Shallot Salsa Verde (page 35)

Charred Scallion Spoon Sauce (page 37)

Garlicky Yogurt Sauce (page 32)

Optional Add-Ons

Crusty bread

A Simple Salad (page 53)

Special Diets

PLANNING ADVICE

- Marinated beans can be made up to one day in advance, just be sure to take them out of the fridge at least 1 hour before serving so that the olive oil isn't congealed.

- The lamb should sit with salt, pepper, and rosemary on it as long as possible. For optimal flavor, rub it one day, then chill it in the fridge overnight, cook it the next day, and then chill it in the fridge again until ready to serve, up to 1 whole day.

- If you're not quite ready when your guests arrive, put them to work slicing tomatoes for the salad.

- Leftover lamb loin roast makes excellent sandwiches, and it is also great sliced into strips and tossed into salads, so don't worry if you made too much.

- If making Pickled Shallot Salsa Verde, keep the pickled shallots separate from the herb oil mixture until just before serving so that the herbs don't brown.

- The Charred Scallion Spoon Sauce and Garlicky Yogurt Sauce can be made up to 1 day in advance and chilled.

> ### For Other Dietary Restrictions
>
> *To feed a vegetarian guest, make sure you add on a green salad and bread, and then make your vegetarian friend a special little plate of planks of feta drizzled with olive oil and sprinkled with herbs and maybe some Aleppo-style pepper flakes or Urfa biber.*
>
> *To feed a vegan guest, forget about that feta and make them a nice slab of toast topped with vegan mayo and sliced tomatoes.*
>
> *To feed a dairy-free guest, don't serve the yogurt sauce.*

COLD ROSEMARY-ROASTED LAMB LOIN

A couple sprigs of rosemary

1 (about 2½-pound/1.2-kg) lamb loin roast, tied (boneless saddle roast)

Olive oil

Kosher salt and freshly ground black pepper

Flaky sea salt

SERVES 4 TO 6, RECIPE EASILY DOUBLED TO SERVE 8 TO 10

Finely chop the rosemary, then rub the lamb roast with a little bit of olive oil (about 1 tablespoon) and sprinkle it on all sides with the rosemary, salt, and pepper. Let it sit for at least 1 hour at room temperature, or wrap it up and tuck it in the fridge overnight. Remove it from the fridge about 1 hour before roasting to bring the meat up toward room temperature so that it cooks more evenly.

Arrange a rack in the middle of the oven and heat to 300°F (150°C).

In a large ovenproof (preferably cast iron) skillet, heat 1 tablespoon of olive oil over medium-high and then sear the roast, turning occasionally, until nicely browned on all sides, about 10 minutes. (If you're doubling this recipe and making two, sear them one at a time.)

Transfer the skillet to the oven and roast, turning the lamb once halfway through, until an instant-read thermometer inserted in the center registers 160°F (71°C) for medium, about 70 minutes (start checking it after 50 minutes). When I'm serving this lamb cold, I cook it to medium because rare meat is just a little weird to me when it's cold. (If you'd like to serve it hot, go ahead and pull it out at 145°F [63°C], then let it rest for 10 minutes before slicing.) Let cool to room temperature, then tightly wrap in plastic or a resealable plastic bag and chill in the fridge until ready to serve.

About 30 minutes before serving, pull the roast out of the fridge to let it warm up a bit. Immediately before serving, thinly slice it (be sure to remove the butcher's twine first!) and arrange it on a large platter or cutting board. There may be some big hunks of cold fat here and there—go ahead and discard those. Drizzle your platter of meat with some of your best olive oil, then sprinkle it with flaky sea salt and a few cranks of black pepper. If serving with Pickled Shallot Salsa Verde (page 35), drizzle some over the top, and serve more alongside.

MARINATED WHITE BEAN AND TOMATO SALAD

½ cup (120 ml) olive oil

4 cloves garlic, thinly sliced

2 (15.5-ounce/439-g) cans white beans, such as butter beans or cannellini, drained and rinsed

Zest of 1 lemon, finely grated

2 sprigs oregano, leaves removed (about 1 tablespoon fresh oregano leaves, or 2 tablespoons dried oregano)

Kosher salt

2 pints (580 g) cherry tomatoes or a couple large heirloom tomatoes, or a mix of shapes and sizes

SERVES 4 TO 6, RECIPE
EASILY DOUBLED TO
SERVE 8 TO 10

In a small pot or skillet, place the oil and garlic and heat over medium-low until the garlic is just barely starting to turn golden brown and smells fragrant, about 5 minutes. In a large bowl or resealable container, place the drained beans, pour the hot garlic oil over, and toss to combine. Add the lemon zest and oregano and season to taste with salt. Let sit at least 1 hour at room temperature, or seal and transfer to the fridge overnight. About 1 hour before serving, remove from the fridge to bring up to room temperature so that the oil isn't cold and congealed.

At 30 minutes or 1 hour before serving, halve the cherry tomatoes (or cut the heirlooms into big bite-size pieces or wedges) and season liberally with salt. This helps intensify the tomato flavor—please don't skip this step. Let them sit in a separate bowl from the beans until just before ready to serve, then lift the tomatoes out (leaving the juices behind) and toss them into the beans. Taste and adjust seasoning as needed. If you want it to taste brighter, add a splash of sherry or red wine vinegar, and maybe add a few fresh oregano leaves. If you want a bit of spice, sprinkle in some crushed red pepper flakes. If it needs salt, you know what to do. Transfer to a serving platter.

A DINNER OF GRILLED CHICKEN AND PEPPERS

Both platters in this sort of Spanish-inspired menu feature a favorite summertime trick of mine: the post-grill marinade. Tossing a very simply seasoned something or other straight onto the grill and then straight into an awaiting punchy dressing adds another level of brightness to earthy, charred grilled goods. It also means less advance prep, and a more leisurely lead-up to serving time. Your finished food can sit in its post-grill marinade for 10 minutes or 2 hours, depending on how your evening is going and when you're ready to eat. While the temperature of the food will decrease as it sits, the flavor will increase, so either way you'll be serving something good.

Party Size

Serves 8 to 10, recipes easily halved to serve 4 to 5 or quartered to serve 2

Sauces to Serve
(pick one!)

Aioli (page 41)

Tahini Sauce (page 42)

Optional Add-Ons

Crusty Bread

A Simple Salad (page 53)

A plate of sliced heirloom tomatoes seasoned with salt

Special Diets

PLANNING ADVICE

- The chicken can be rubbed up to a day in advance, but it will also still be good if you rub it 30 minutes before grilling. Really, it's about what fits into your schedule better.

- Whichever sauce you choose, it can be made 1 day in advance and chilled. If the aioli solidifies in the fridge, just whisk in a bit of water before serving to loosen it.

- This menu makes excellent leftovers. Cut cold leftover chicken off the bone and into pieces and toss it with the leftover peppers and you've got yourself a great chicken salad for lunch. Stir in some greens if you like.

For Other Dietary Restrictions

For a vegan or vegetarian guest, throw your favorite brand of veggie or bean burger on the grill—it'll be excellent topped with the peppers.

To serve a pescatarian, rub a swordfish steak in salt and smoked paprika, lightly coat in olive oil, and grill over medium-high until opaque and lightly charred, about 4 minutes per side.

GRILLED PAPRIKA CHICKEN WITH GARLIC VINEGAR

For the chicken

3 tablespoons kosher salt

2 tablespoons smoked paprika

1 tablespoon freshly ground black pepper

½ teaspoon ground cayenne

7 to 8 pounds (3.2 to 3.6 kg) bone-in, skin-on chicken parts (choose a mix of drumsticks, thighs, and breasts, or stick with just one type)

For the garlic vinegar

8 large cloves garlic, finely chopped

1 cup (240 ml) sherry or red wine vinegar

2 teaspoons kosher salt

2 teaspoons white or brown sugar

SERVES 8 TO 10, RECIPE EASILY HALVED TO SERVE 4 TO 5 OR QUARTERED TO SERVE 2

RUB THE CHICKEN

In a large bowl, stir the salt, paprika, pepper, and cayenne together. Add the chicken pieces and toss to coat thoroughly. Let sit about 30 minutes before grilling for the rub flavors to sink in, or cover and refrigerate for up to 1 day before grilling.

MAKE THE GARLIC VINEGAR

In a small bowl, stir together the garlic, vinegar, salt, and sugar and let sit at least 30 minutes and up to 3 hours for the garlic to infuse the vinegar with flavor.

GRILL THE CHICKEN

Prepare a grill for two-zone heat. (For a charcoal grill, push two-thirds of the coals over to one side of the grill and scatter the remaining third of the coals over the other side. And for a gas grill, set one side of the burners to high heat and the other side to medium-low.)

Arrange the chicken pieces, skin side down, over the hottest part of the grates and grill, turning halfway through, until lightly charred on all sides, 5 to 10 minutes. Move the chicken to the cooler part of the grates, cover with the lid, and continue to grill, turning several times (keep covered), until an instant-read thermometer inserted into the thickest part registers 160°F (71°C) for breasts and 155°F (68°C) for thighs and drumsticks, 15 to 25 minutes longer. (The chicken temperature will increase by about 5 degrees as it rests.) Transfer the chicken pieces to a large serving platter as they are done (smaller pieces will go more quickly). As soon as the last piece is done, pour about half of the garlic vinegar evenly over the top of the chicken and let sit 5 to 10 minutes before serving. Serve the remaining garlic vinegar alongside.

CHARRED AND MARINATED SWEET AND SHISHITO PEPPERS

Neutral oil, such as
   sunflower, safflower, or
   grapeseed, for the grill
1 pound (455 g) sweet mini
   peppers
1 red onion, cut into 2-inch
   (5-cm) wedges
3 pints (477 g) shishito
   peppers
½ cup (120 ml) olive oil
3 tablespoons sherry or red
   wine vinegar
Kosher salt and freshly
   ground black pepper
1 cup (30 g) parsley leaves

SERVES 8 TO 10, RECIPE
EASILY HALVED TO SERVE
4 TO 5 OR QUARTERED
TO SERVE 2

Prepare a grill for medium-high heat (or use the hotter side of a grill set up for two-zone grilling); oil the grate. Grill the sweet peppers and onion wedges, turning often, until lightly charred and softened, about 5 minutes. Transfer to a bowl and cover to keep warm and help the peppers continue to soften as they steam in the bowl. Rub more oil on the grate and grill the shishito peppers, turning often, until lightly charred and softened, about 3 minutes. Transfer to the bowl with the sweet peppers and onions. Add the olive oil, vinegar, 1 teaspoon salt, and ½ teaspoon pepper and toss to coat. Cover and let marinate for at least 10 minutes and up to 1 hour. Just before serving, stir in the parsley, taste, and add more salt if needed, then transfer to a serving platter.

A MUSTARD PORK ROAST
AND WEDGE SALAD DINNER

This menu features three of my favorite little helpers: anchovies, the food processor, and the slow cooker. Have I told you yet about how much I love anchovies? I sneak them into as many things as I can to boost and funk up flavors (just as long as there aren't vegetarians at my table). The food processor can be a mini prep (in fact, I prefer my mini prep for this) or a full size—either way it turns the task of making a flavor-packed (hi anchovies!) paste to rub all over the pork roast a day or two in advance into a breeze, and it helps you make a homemade mayo-based Caesar-style dressing as easy as pressing a button. The slow cooker is my favorite tool for cooking big hunks of meat without turning on the oven and heating the kitchen in the summer, and I'm sorry to all you Instant Pot fans out there, but I just love my slow cooker. I like that I can open it up and poke at the meat and know exactly what's happening. Anyway, this menu will also work in the oven if you're into that, but why turn on the oven in the summer?

Party Size
Serves 8 to 10

Party Prep
At least 2 days of advance prep are required.

Sauce to Serve (choose one!)
Pickled Shallot Salsa Verde (page 35)

Pickled Peppercorn Vinaigrette (page 51)

Optional Add-Ons
Bread

A platter of sliced heirloom tomatoes seasoned with salt

Special Diets

PLANNING ADVICE

- Marinate the pork at least overnight and up to 2 days before slow-cooking.

- The pork cooks in the slow cooker for almost 8 hours, but it can be cooked up to a whole day before serving.

- Prep the lettuce wedges a few hours in advance; refrigerate them wrapped in a damp clean towel.

- The salad dressing can be made up to 1 day in advance and stored in the fridge. Pull it out of the fridge at least 30 minutes before serving to let it warm up just a bit so it's easier to drizzle over the top of the little gem wedges.

- Either sauce can be made a few hours before serving. If making Pickled Shallot Salsa Verde, keep the pickled shallots separate from the herb oil mixture until just before serving so that the herbs don't brown.

For Other Dietary Restrictions

To serve a dairy-free guest, don't add the Parm to the salad dressing: It'll still taste good. You'll need to add a bit more salt or maybe a couple more anchovies to give it extra oomph and body.

To serve a vegetarian guest, make the dressing without anchovies, pour some out for them, and then add the anchovies to the dressing for everyone else and stir extra Parm into your vegetarian's stash. Serve them their own salad, and assemble a quick hummus bowl topped with fresh cucumbers and tomatoes.

To serve a vegan guest, do the same as above, but make the dressing without the Parm.

SLOW-COOKER PORK ROAST

6 anchovy fillets

6 cloves garlic

¼ cup (60 ml) Dijon mustard, preferably but not necessarily country-style (grainy)

2 tablespoons kosher salt

1 tablespoon light brown sugar

1 teaspoon freshly ground black pepper

¼ teaspoon ground allspice

1 (approximately 6-pound/2.7-kg) boneless pork shoulder (Boston butt) roast, tied (Ask your butcher to tie it for you.)

Handful of chopped fresh herbs, such as flat-leaf parsley or cilantro (optional)

SERVES 8 TO 10

Pulse the anchovies, garlic, mustard, salt, sugar, pepper, and allspice in the jar of a food processor until a thick paste forms. Rub that paste all over your tied pork roast, pushing it between the cracks as much as possible. (If you care about how your hands smell, you might want to wear gloves for this process.)

I use a 4-quart (3.8-L) slow cooker for this recipe because it's the only one I have and the pork roast just barely fits into it, which means the pork very quickly gets submerged in a bath of its own fat—a good thing for a pork roast to do. But you can use whatever size you have. If you have room to store the insert of your slow cooker in the fridge, tuck the rubbed roast into it, cover it, and refrigerate. If there's just no room, seal it into a resealable plastic bag and then refrigerate. Let it sit at least overnight or up to 2 days so that the salt and seasonings in the paste have a chance to penetrate the meat to tenderize and flavor it.

Place the insert and the pork into your slow cooker set to low, cover, and cook until the meat is fork-tender but not completely falling apart, 7 to 7½ hours. (If it's done cooking before you're ready for it, simply remove it from the cooker, wrap it tightly in foil, and let it sit for up to 2 hours, then re-warm—still wrapped!— in a 300°F (150°C) oven before slicing.) Transfer to a cutting board and let rest 5 to 10 minutes. Remove the butcher's twine, then slice and transfer to a serving platter. Drizzle whichever sauce you're using over the top, or strain some of the juice out of the slow cooker, drizzle that over the top instead, and toss a flurry of chopped herbs over the top to make it pretty.

TO ROAST IN THE OVEN

Place the pork in a large Dutch oven, cover, and roast in a 300°F (150°C) oven, basting occasionally, until the meat is fork-tender, 6 to 7 hours.

LITTLE GEM CAESAR WEDGES

5 heads little gem lettuce
(or romaine hearts, if you
can't find little gem)

8 anchovy fillets

2 egg yolks

1 teaspoon smooth Dijon
mustard

2 teaspoons lemon juice

½ cup (120 ml) neutral
oil, such as sunflower,
safflower, or grapeseed

1 cup (100 g) finely grated
Parmesan cheese

2 tablespoons white wine
vinegar

Coarsely ground black
pepper

1 cup (115 g) store-bought
crispy fried shallots

SERVES 8 TO 10, EASILY
HALVED TO SERVE 4 TO 5

Trim the base of each little gem lettuce just to remove the brown part—you want the core intact. Remove and discard any bruised or mushy outer leaves, then cut each head into quarters lengthwise through the center of the core. Gently rinse the wedges in cold water, drain, then lay out on a towel-lined sheet pan to air dry. Once dry, wrap in a damp clean dish towel and store in the fridge until ready to serve (up to 4 hours in advance of serving).

In the jar of a food processor (I love to use my mini food processor for this), pulse the anchovies, egg yolks, mustard, and lemon juice until mostly smooth. Slowly stream in the oil with the processor running until thick and creamy. Add the Parm, vinegar, and 1 teaspoon of pepper and pulse until combined. Taste, and adjust the seasoning as needed.

Arrange the little gem wedges in a single layer on a large serving platter. Drizzle the dressing evenly over all the wedges, then top with the crispy fried shallots and black pepper.

A QUICK WAY TO SERVE GRILLED STEAK AND MELON SALAD FOR DINNER

I like to serve this one on a Friday or on the first night I arrive at my family's lake house with a group of friends—it's so summery and festive, and it sets the mood for a fun-filled weekend while still being easy enough to pull together after a long workday or day of driving. I had to stop myself from adding tomatoes and melon to every single menu in this summer chapter. But please, add a platter of melon anywhere you can all summer long: as a snack (I've got some ideas for you over on page 22), as a dessert, or as a side. Any kind of melon is always better with some acid and some salt. Some of the salt in the melon salad in this menu comes from fish sauce, which you can also smugly reveal is the secret ingredient when your guests all exclaim: "Why is this so good!?" Since we've got the fish sauce out, put it in the steak marinade as well and it adds a funky depth and oomph that is a very good thing, and often used in Vietnamese grilled meat marinades. This punchy, quick-soak marinade is flavored with lemongrass and ginger in a sweet, nutty coconut milk base. The marinade also works great for boneless skinless chicken thighs, if you'd rather not cook steak.

Party Size	Sauce to Serve	Special Diets
Serves 6 to 8, recipes easily halved to serve 2 to 4 or doubled to serve 12 to 14	Crispy Garlic and Chili Oil (page 36)	

Party Prep

No advance prep is required; the full menu can be prepped and served within an hour or two.

Optional Add-Ons

Grilled or boiled corn on the cob

Rice

A Simple Salad (page 53)

PLANNING ADVICE

- With an extra set of hands helping so that one person can grill, and so one person can prep the salad and any add-ons, this is a party menu that can be made in less than an hour.

- Making the melon salad is a good group activity for guests who want to help: Have them divide and conquer prepping different ingredients for it.

- The steak marinade can be made a day in advance, but the steak only wants to sit in it for about 1 hour tops—too much time in this powerful marinade and the meat starts to break down.

- If you want to serve the Crispy Garlic and Chili Oil (and I think you should!), make it a couple days or at least a couple hours ahead of time so you won't have to play host while also trying not to burn the garlic at the same time.

> ### For Other Dietary Restrictions
>
> *To serve a vegetarian or vegan guest, add corn or rice to the menu and omit the fish sauce from the marinade and the salad. Reserve some of the marinade before it goes on the steak and use it to brush a halved and cross-hatched zucchini for each vegan or veggie guest, then grill until tender and lightly charred.*

LEMONGRASS-GINGER COCONUT GRILLED STEAK

3 pounds (1.4 kg) skirt steak, cut into 6-inch (15-cm) pieces

3 teaspoons kosher salt

1 cup (240 ml) coconut milk

1 stalk lemongrass, smashed and coarsely chopped

1 (3-inch/7.5-cm) piece ginger, peeled and finely chopped (3 tablespoons)

2 cloves garlic, crushed and coarsely chopped

1 teaspoon brown sugar

1 tablespoon fish sauce

Flaky sea salt, for serving

SERVES 6 TO 8, RECIPE EASILY HALVED TO SERVE 2 TO 4 OR DOUBLED TO SERVE 12 TO 14

Season the steak on all sides with the salt and place in a baking dish.

In the jar of a blender or food processor, pulse the coconut milk, lemongrass, ginger, garlic, sugar, and fish sauce until as smooth as possible—it will never get totally smooth with all that tough lemongrass fiber, but that's alright. Pour over the steak, turn to coat, and let sit at least 30 minutes and up to 1 hour. (You can make the marinade mixture up to 1 day in advance, just store it in the fridge and give it a good stir before pouring over your steak since the coconut fat may have separated and solidified.)

Prepare a grill for high-heat grilling. Grill the steak pieces, turning once halfway through, until deeply charred, 3 to 4 minutes per side. Let sit 10 minutes before slicing against the grain. Cutting the skirt steak against the grain is very important to make your eating experience pleasant, but the shape of a skirt steak is made to trick you. You might think you should cut it into strips crosswise, but think again: Turn your section of skirt steak so that the stripes of the grain go side to side in front of you instead of up and down, and then slice it into strips *through* those stripes, which will mean you're cutting it lengthwise. You can also turn it on the diagonal and cut sort of lengthwise on a bias, as long as you're cutting *against* the grain.

Assemble the sliced steak on a serving platter and drizzle lightly with Crispy Garlic and Chili Oil, if using, or just sprinkle it with flaky sea salt. You could also sprinkle it with some chile flakes if you want to add spice but didn't get around to making the Crispy Garlic and Chili Oil.

MELON, CUCUMBER, AND AVOCADO SALAD

1 pound (455 g) mini seedless (Persian) cucumbers, sliced ¼ inch (6 mm) thick either on the bias for ovals or straight across for coins

1 teaspoon kosher salt, plus more to taste

¼ cup (60 ml) lime juice

2 teaspoons fish sauce (Optional, but highly recommended—I promise it doesn't make this taste fishy.)

½ honeydew or cantaloupe melon, cut into 1 to 2-inch (2.5 to 5-cm) pieces of whatever shape you like

2 avocados, peeled and sliced into ½-inch (12-mm) wedges

1 cup (30 g) basil leaves, mint leaves, and/or cilantro leaves and tender stems

SERVES 6 TO 8, RECIPE EASILY HALVED TO SERVE 2 TO 4 OR DOUBLED TO SERVE 12 TO 14

In a large bowl, toss the cucumbers in 1 teaspoon of salt and set aside for at least 5 minutes and up to 20 minutes. In a small bowl, stir together the lime juice and fish sauce and give it a little taste. If it's not salty enough, add a pinch of salt.

Just before you're ready to serve dinner, add the melon to the cucumber, pour the dressing over, and toss to combine. Then add the avocado and whatever herbs you're using (you want to add these two things last so the avocado doesn't mush all over everything and your herbs don't wilt), and use your hands to very gently toss everything together. Still using your hands, transfer the salad to a large serving platter, gently lifting and placing, leaving any remaining dressing behind in the bowl to discard.

A VACATION-READY GRILLED FISH AND CORN BOIL DINNER

The corn dish on this menu is sort of like a clam boil without the seafood in it, with some quickly charred seafood on the side. It tastes like a seaside view, and is ready for summer on the deck or patio, no matter what your view is. If you've got a grill, grill the fish; it's just more fun. But the rest of the menu doesn't require a grill, so go ahead and pan-sear the fish if that's easier for you.

Party Size	Sauce to Serve	Special Diets
Serves 6 to 8, recipes easily halved to serve 3 to 4	Charred Scallion Spoon Sauce (page 37)	

Party Prep

Very little advance prep is required; the full menu can be prepped and served within an hour or two.

Optional Add-Ons

A Simple Salad (page 53)

PLANNING ADVICE

- The miso butter can be made up to 5 days in advance; let come to room temperature for at least 1 hour before serving.

- If swordfish steaks are hard to find or not to your taste, try salmon steaks instead. If you don't want to have fish but you want to grill some kind of steak, the menu works with pork steaks too—use the pork steak recipe from page 66.

For Other Dietary Restrictions

To serve a vegetarian guest, grill (or pan-sear) some eggplant steaks before you do the fish and top them with the same Charred Scallion Spoon Sauce.

To serve a dairy-free guest, set aside some of the corn, potatoes, and green beans without the miso butter and top them with the Charred Scallion Spoon Sauce instead.

To serve a vegan guest, do both of the above.

GRILLED SWORDFISH STEAKS

Neutral oil for grill such as sunflower, safflower, or grapeseed

4 swordfish steaks, about 1 inch (2.5 cm) thick (about 3½ pounds/100 g total), cut in half

Kosher salt and freshly ground black pepper

2 tablespoons olive oil, for pan searing, plus more for serving

Flaky sea salt, for serving

SERVES 6 TO 8, RECIPE EASILY HALVED TO SERVE 3 TO 4

IF GRILLING THE SWORDFISH STEAKS

Prepare a grill for medium-high heat; lightly oil the grate with neutral oil.

While the grill heats, pat the swordfish dry and season all over with salt and pepper. Place on a sheet pan and let sit at room temperature for 15 minutes, which helps the fish absorb the seasoning and warm up a bit so that it cooks more evenly. Rub the swordfish all over with 2 tablespoons of the neutral oil to prevent them from sticking to the grill and to encourage browning. Grill the steaks, resisting the urge to move them around, until grill marks appear, about 4 minutes. Carefully turn the steaks over and grill until the fish is opaque all the way through, 2 to 4 minutes.

Transfer to a platter and drizzle with the Charred Scallion Spoon Sauce (page 37), if using, or just olive oil and flaky sea salt, if not.

IF PAN-SEARING THE SWORDFISH STEAKS

Pat the swordfish dry and season all over with salt and pepper. Place on a sheet pan and let sit at room temperature for 15 minutes, which helps the fish absorb the seasoning and warm up a bit so that it cooks more evenly.

Heat the olive oil in a large nonstick or cast-iron skillet over medium-high. Working in batches if needed, cook the steaks, flipping often, until the fish is opaque and firm to the touch, 5 to 6 minutes.

Transfer to a platter and drizzle with the Charred Scallion Spoon Sauce (page 37), if using, or just olive oil and flaky sea salt, if not.

ONE-POT POTATOES, GREEN BEANS, AND CORN WITH MISO-PEPPER BUTTER

For the butter

¾ cup (1½ sticks/170 g) unsalted butter, at room temperature

3 tablespoons white miso

2 teaspoons Aleppo-style pepper flakes or 1½ teaspoons crushed red pepper flakes

2 teaspoons freshly ground black pepper

Kosher salt

For the potatoes

Kosher salt

3 pounds (1.4 kg) baby new potatoes

1 pound (455 g) green beans, trimmed

6 ears corn on the cob, shucked and broken in half

SERVES 6 TO 8, RECIPE EASILY HALVED TO SERVE 3 TO 4

MAKE THE BUTTER

In the bowl of a food processor, pulse the butter, miso, pepper flakes, pepper, and 1 teaspoon salt until smooth. If you don't have a food processor or don't want to get yours dirty (I know it's annoying to wash), simply mix vigorously by hand in a large bowl with a wooden spoon. It takes more muscle, but it works just as well. Transfer the butter mixture to a small bowl and let sit at room temperature for up to 2 hours before serving, or cover and chill for up to 5 days. If making in advance, be sure to let come to room temperature before serving.

MAKE THE POTATOES

Place the potatoes in a large pot of salted water and bring to a boil over medium heat. Continue boiling until the potatoes are just fork-tender, about 12 minutes. Add the green beans and corn pieces and continue cooking until the green beans are crisp-tender, about 5 minutes more. If your pot isn't big enough or if you're doubling this recipe to serve more people, do the potatoes and green beans together, and get a separate pot going for the corn. Drain everything, transfer to a large serving platter, and dot with about a third of the miso butter (scoop it out with a small spoon or butter knife). Toss and dot with about a third of the butter again. Serve additional butter alongside.

A VERY SUMMERY GRILLED VEGGIES AND TOMATO SALAD DINNER

Quickly grilled vegetables tossed over yogurt sauce, or blue cheese tossed with tomatoes and herbs—this is the kind of low-effort, high-reward food that summer is famous for, so you can spend less time cooking and more time lingering over the table, preferably out in the backyard if you have one. I love to add my Skillet Socca (page 28) to this menu because it serves as bread but also as an extra protein source, but you do have to turn on the oven to make it, so seriously, no pressure.

Party Size

Serves 6 to 8, recipes easily halved to serve 2 to 4 or doubled to serve 12 to 14

Party Prep

No advance prep required; the full menu can be made in about an hour.

Sauces to Serve
(choose one or two)

Garlicky Yogurt Sauce (page 32)

Tahini Sauce (page 42)

Blender Spiced Green Sauce (page 43)

Optional Add-ons

Skillet Socca (page 28) or store-bought flatbread or pita

A Simple Salad (page 53)

Special Diets

PLANNING ADVICE

- Whichever sauce or sauces you choose, they can be made 1 day in advance and chilled.

- Everything else is best made shortly before serving. No one said it all has to be served piping hot though, so don't worry if your vegetables are done grilling before you're ready to eat.

- Slicing tomatoes, herbs, and cheese for the salad is a good group activity—put your friends to work helping you pull that off while you drink spritzes.

For Other Dietary Restrictions

To feed a vegan or dairy-free guest, simply reserve some of the grilled vegetables for them before you put the rest on top of yogurt sauce, and give them their own plate of tomato salad without cheese in it. Maybe add some canned beans to that salad so they get a bit of protein, or serve them extra socca.

ZA'ATAR GRILLED EGGPLANT AND ZUCCHINI

4 medium zucchinis (about
3 pounds/1.4 kg),
quartered lengthwise into
wedges

2 medium or 4 small
eggplants (about
1 pound/455 g), cut
lengthwise into 1-inch
(2.5-cm) wedges

½ cup (120 ml) olive oil, plus
more for grilling and
drizzling

2 tablespoons za'atar

Kosher salt and freshly
ground black pepper

Flaky sea salt, for serving

SERVES 6 TO 8, RECIPE
EASILY HALVED TO SERVE
2 TO 4 OR DOUBLED TO
SERVE 12 TO 14

Prepare a grill for medium heat. In a large bowl, toss the zucchini, eggplant, and ½ cup (120 ml) of the oil; season with the za'atar, 2 teaspoons of salt, and 1 teaspoon of pepper and toss to coat thoroughly. Working in batches if needed, grill the zucchini and eggplant wedges, turning often, until steamy, tender, and charred all over, 8 to 12 minutes. Return to the large bowl.

Spread the yogurt, tahini, or spiced green sauce, if using, evenly on a large serving platter, then pile the grilled vegetables on top. If not using any sauces, or if you'd like to keep them on the side, simply pile the grilled vegetables on a large serving platter. Drizzle with olive oil and sprinkle with flaky sea salt before serving.

BLUE CHEESE, TOMATO, AND HERB SALAD

4 pounds (1.8 kg) mixed
   heirloom tomatoes
   (preferably various colors
   and sizes), sliced into
   ¼-inch (6-mm) thick
   rounds, or halved if small
Kosher salt and freshly
   ground black pepper
½ cup (120 ml) olive oil
1 tablespoon sherry vinegar
   or red wine vinegar
½ pound (225 g) mild and
   firm blue cheese, sliced
   into shards
1 cup (30 g) dill fronds
1 cup (30 g) parsley and/or
   mint leaves
¼ cup (11 g) finely snipped
   chives

SERVES 6 TO 8, RECIPE
EASILY HALVED TO SERVE
2 TO 4 OR DOUBLED TO
SERVE 12 TO 14

Place the tomatoes on a large serving platter and season all over with 1 teaspoon salt and ½ teaspoon pepper, then drizzle with the oil and vinegar and let sit at least 10 minutes.

Add the cheese and herbs to the platter of tomatoes and nudge gently to combine. Taste and season with more salt and pepper if desired.

SWEETS FOR SHARING

Dessert is a very good reason to keep sitting around the table talking after dinner. It also makes you happy. And as the last thing served, it's most likely to be the thing your guests remember first. And so naturally, I believe there should always be dessert. But that doesn't mean you need to actually make a dessert—just pass around something sweet to share. When I have time, I love to bake a cake to present on a cake stand, especially if there's been a recent birthday, so I can stick candles in it and embarrass the birthday guest with a singing cake procession. I prefer the communal nature and opportunities for seconds of a dessert that's divisible rather than individual, with just two notable creamy exceptions, as you will see. What follows are my favorite sweets to share at the end of a meal, in order from zero to medium effort (though nothing here is actually that hard). And of course, they're all naturally gluten-free, but no one will ever notice.

FOR THE TABLE

THE "NOTHING FOR DESSERT" STRATEGY, FOUR WAYS

When I have a day or two to prepare for a dinner party, the dessert is the first thing I make. And from one messy baker to another, I recommend you do too, if time allows. If time does not allow for even a morning-of bake, don't make a thing. You'll just stress yourself out. Instead, call on your pantry for a no-recipe, no-fuss sweet ending to the meal. Here's four ways I like to do it.

#1 CHOCOLATE PLUS

Find whatever chocolate you have in your pantry (it's worth it to always keep some good stuff in there) and break it up into pieces and scatter it on a plate. Drizzle a little of your best olive oil over the top and sprinkle with flaky salt. If you're feeling spicy, add some mild Aleppo-style pepper flakes too. Present it with a flourish (and some drinks, see page 251). That's all. But you don't have to stop there—add a plate of berries too, or a plate of sliced fruit. Or a bowl of cherries in summer, or clementines in winter. Or add a bowl of salted nuts or dried fruit. Whatever tidbits you have in your pantry that are conducive to snacking on while sipping an after-dinner drink can be added to your chocolate spread. And suddenly it feels like you made dessert, doesn't it?

#2 YOU CAN STILL WHIP CREAM

An unopened pint of heavy cream stays fresh for several months in the fridge, so I always have at least one tucked in the back, just in case. Even if you didn't bake something to whip cream for, make the whipped cream the main event. Make Communal Whipped Cream (see page 229) and add a little bit of maple syrup or white sugar at the end. Dollop it over bowls of fresh berries or sliced fruit. Or over ice cream, or both. Or whisk in a little brandy and/or dessert wine along with sugar, drape it into elegant bowls, and you've got the very British dessert syllabub, ready to eat with a spoon. Sprinkle some cinnamon or lemon zest on top if you want to make it look more like you planned it.

#3 HOT DATES AND NUTS

Heat some olive oil in a heavy skillet and toss in some whole fresh Medjool dates and any kind of nuts you have handy. Add a sprig of rosemary or thyme if you have some, and maybe a few peels of orange zest, or a sprinkle of Aleppo-style pepper flakes. Keep cooking, stirring often, until the dates are lightly charred and the nuts are toasty and fragrant. Transfer to a plate, top with flaky sea salt, and pass around with cognac, amaro, or your favorite whiskey. If you don't have nuts or if someone is allergic, skip them. For me this is really all about the dates—I love how they get super crispy on the outside and hot and gooey on the inside. Proceed with jokes about my dating life as you must, but do go ahead and try those hot dates on top of cold vanilla ice cream, with your best olive oil and flaky salt on top of both. These are also excellent served with cheese.

#4 CHEESE CAN COUNT AS DESSERT

But you don't need to make Hot Dates and Nuts—cheese can hold its own for dessert. We all know in France the cheese comes between dinner and dessert. Well, I like to make it the main event, with a few sweet-ish accompaniments to end a meal. Put out a cheese or two with some honey and apples, or a jar of jam. No crackers or bread needed, but help yourself if you'd like them. Just be sure (especially if serving a soft cheese) to pull it out of the fridge before dinner so it has time to warm before serving.

COMMUNAL WHIPPED CREAM

*If someone at the table gets too into whipping and your cream becomes too stiff, gently beat more cold heavy cream into the whipped cream, bit by bit, until it's reached the ideal billowy, soft texture.

Every baked good in this book is very happy to be served with a dollop of unsweetened whipped cream. When I serve whipped cream at a dinner party, I turn it into a group activity, and I promise, it's fun. Pour a pint (2 cups/480 ml) of cold heavy cream into your biggest bowl, add your biggest whisk, and pass it to a friend. No one keeps the bowl for long—a few beats of the whisk and pass it on. By the time it gets all the way around the table the cream should be holding nice soft peaks. It's usually hilarious, gets everyone awake and involved, and takes one task off your plate. When the cream is whipped but not too stiff,* stir in a tiny pinch of salt and a splash of vanilla extract, or sometimes a splash of brandy, and trade the whisk for a serving spoon. (At this point in the night there are usually too many dirty dishes in piles in my kitchen to consider transferring the whipped cream to a serving bowl, but by all means, feel free to do so.)

1 pint of heavy cream makes about 4 cups (960 ml) of whipped cream, which serves about 10 people. Divide or increase as necessary to serve your crowd—whipped cream doesn't really make good leftovers.

ONE-BOWL OLIVE OIL ALMOND CAKE

½ cup (125ml) olive oil, plus
　　more for pan

4 large eggs

1 cup (200 g) granulated
　　sugar

2 cups (230 g) almond flour

½ cup gluten-free or regular
　　all-purpose flour (68 g)

2 teaspoons baking powder

1 teaspoon kosher salt

Juice and zest of 1 lemon,
　　finely grated

¼ teaspoon almond extract

MAKES ONE 9-INCH (23 CM)
CAKE; SERVES 8 TO 10

Baking really can't get easier than this gluten- and dairy-free cake. You can make this cake without any special equipment, and the recipe is easy enough to memorize, so you can make it anywhere you go in the world when you need a cake. If you don't know what kind of food restrictions you're catering to, chances are you'll be safe with this cake. (Unless of course there's a nut allergy—please do ask if anyone has a nut allergy before serving almond cake.) This cake is good on its own, but it's even more exciting with something spooned on top. I'm not much of a frosting person, but if you are, this is a cake you can frost. Whipped cream, though? Always! Add some fruit too if it's in season. Strawberries? Raspberries? Sliced peaches or apricots? All are good. Toss them in a bit of sugar and let them sit for at least 10 minutes to get syrupy before passing the bowl around for each guest to top their cake as they like.

Preheat the oven to 350°F (175°C). Line the bottom of a 9-inch (23-cm) cake pan with parchment, then grease the pan and parchment lightly with olive oil.

In a large bowl or in the bowl of a stand mixer fitted with the whisk attachment, whisk together the eggs and sugar until pale. You can totally make this cake without a mixer, but if you've got one and you want to use it, go for it. Gradually start streaming in the olive oil, whisking while you go. This is kind of like making mayonnaise or aioli—you want the batter to emulsify, not separate, so don't add the oil too quickly. That is the hardest part. Now add the almond flour, flour, baking powder, salt, lemon juice and zest, and almond extract and whisk just until combined. Transfer your batter to the prepared cake pan and smooth the top.

Bake until the top is golden brown and springs back easily when gently pressed with a finger, 30 to 35 minutes. Let cool for 10 minutes in the cake pan, then invert onto a plate to get it out of the pan. Invert once more onto a cooling rack to let the cake cool completely with its pretty top side facing up.

The cake keeps for up to 4 days, covered at room temperature.

ALMOST-ANY-FRUIT SKILLET CRISP

For the filling

About 8 cups (1 kg) sliced fruit or berries (No need to peel anything; cut larger fruit into either 1-inch [2.5-cm] pieces or ½-inch [12-mm] wedges, as desired.)

¼ cup (55 g) light brown sugar

1 tablespoon lemon juice

1 tablespoon cornstarch (optional; only if using juicy berries or extra-juicy stone fruit)

½ teaspoon cinnamon

Pinch of salt

2 tablespoons unsalted butter

For the crumble topping

1 cup (90 g) rolled oats

¾ cup (165 g) packed light brown sugar

¾ cup (95 g) gluten-free or regular all-purpose flour

¾ cup (85 g) almond flour

1 teaspoon kosher salt

1 teaspoon cinnamon

½ teaspoon baking soda

¼ teaspoon grated nutmeg

¾ cup (1½ sticks/170 g) unsalted butter, at room temperature, cut into small pieces

SERVES 6 TO 8, RECIPE EASILY
HALVED TO SERVE 2 TO 4

This crisp works with almost any fruit or berry you'd like to turn into a crisp—apples, pears, peaches, blueberries, cherries, etc. If using a juicier fruit or berry, like peaches, blueberries, or cherries, you'll want to add a bit of cornstarch to the fruit mixture to help it not be too runny. But the crisp is forgiving, so don't worry too much about it. If it turns out too runny, there's more fruit sauce to eat with spoonfuls of whipped cream.

Preheat the oven to 375°F (190°C).

MAKE THE FILLING

In a large bowl, use your hands to toss the fruit or berries with the brown sugar, lemon juice, cornstarch (if using), cinnamon, and salt until thoroughly coated.

Melt the butter in an ovenproof 10-inch (25-cm) skillet over medium-low heat. Add the fruit and cook, stirring occasionally, until it begins to bubble and exude juices, about 5 minutes. Remove from the heat. I like to start my crisps like this because it ensures that the fruit gets fully cooked and softened before the crisp topping burns. It also helps evaporate some of the water from the fruit before you seal it up with a crust on top, to prevent a runny filling.

MAKE THE CRUMBLE TOPPING

In the same large bowl you used to mix the fruit (no need to wash it!) stir together the oats, brown sugar, flour, almond flour, salt, cinnamon, baking soda, and nutmeg. Add the butter and then squeeze, mix, and crumble the mixture with your fingers until it comes together in little clumps. It should be drier than cookie dough, but hold together when squeezed.

Scatter the crumble all over the top of the warm fruit in the skillet, then transfer to the oven and bake until the topping is golden brown and crispy and the filling is bubbling, about 30 minutes. Let sit at least 10 minutes before serving so no one burns their tongues on the hot crisp, but do serve it warm—preferably with cold whipped cream or vanilla ice cream on top.

VERY WIGGLY YOGURT PANNA COTTA

1 packet gelatin (2½
    teaspoons/7 g)
½ cup (120 ml) cold water
2 cups (480 ml) heavy cream,
    divided
½ cup (100 g) granulated
    sugar
½ teaspoon kosher salt
2½ cups (600 ml) full-fat
    plain yogurt (*not* Greek-
    style)

SERVES 6, RECIPE EASILY
HALVED TO SERVE 3 OR
DOUBLED TO SERVE 12

Here's the thing about panna cotta. If you think you don't like it it's probably because you've never had panna cotta that's wiggly enough. This classic Italian dessert is meant to be just sweet milk set with enough gelatin to hold its shape, jiggling ethereally as you slurp it from your spoon. It's light, cooling, and delicate—and as easy to make as Jell-O. To lean into that cooling light thing, I make mine with yogurt in the mix, which makes it ever so slightly tart. Serve it as is, or drizzle a thin skim of high-quality balsamic vinegar over the top: Trust me, this combo makes me want to dance. Or if it's in season, add a bowl of sliced stone fruit tossed in a bit of sugar to the table for guests to spoon over their puddings as desired.

In a small bowl, sprinkle the gelatin over the water and set aside to bloom.

In a saucepan, heat half of the cream (1 cup/240 ml) with the sugar and salt over medium, stirring, until the sugar is dissolved, about 4 minutes. To make sure the sugar is dissolved, dip a finger into the mixture, then rub it against your thumb— you shouldn't be able to feel any granules. Transfer to a large mixing bowl and stir in the bloomed gelatin until fully dissolved. Then stir in the remaining cream and yogurt until combined. Pour the mixture into six small serving cups or bowls, loosely cover making sure that the cover doesn't touch the pudding, and chill in the fridge or in a cold enclosed garage or porch (below 40°F [4.5°C] and above 32°F [0°C]) until set, at least 8 hours.

HOT SUMMER SPOON CAKE

For the fruit

1 pint (455 g) raspberries,
  blueberries, or
  blackberries; halved
  strawberries; pitted
  and halved cherries;
  halved figs; sliced plums,
  peaches, or nectarines

2 tablespoons granulated
  sugar

Juice and zest of 1 lemon,
  finely grated

For the batter

½ cup (100 g) granulated
  sugar

½ cup (48 g) almond flour

½ cup (64 g) gluten-free or
  regular all-purpose flour

1 teaspoon kosher salt

1 teaspoon baking powder

½ cup (1 stick/115 g) unsalted
  butter

¼ cup (60 ml) whole milk

1 large egg

SERVES 4 TO 6, RECIPE
EASILY DOUBLED TO
SERVE 8 TO 10

You know those late summer nights when it first starts getting just a little bit cold after dark, and you want a dessert that you can serve warm, à la mode? Sure, you could make a summer fruit pie or cobbler and serve it warm, but spoon cake is so much easier. And more fun because it's a cake that you serve with a spoon. It's a warm, gooey, pudding-y kind of cake, and it's just dying to make your vanilla ice cream melt.

Prep the fruit and batter well before dinner, then dump them together and bake the cake as your guests clear the dinner plates. It'll be ready to eat within half an hour.

PREPARE THE FRUIT

In a medium bowl, toss the berries or fruit of choice in the sugar, lemon juice, and zest and let sit at least 30 minutes and up to 4 hours. This is a good thing to do before dinner, so it's ready to go.

MAKE THE BATTER

In a large bowl, stir together the sugar, almond flour, flour, salt, and baking powder, and set aside. (Do this in advance before dinner too!)

When ready to make dessert, turn on the oven to 400°F (205°C). Place the butter in a 1½ to 2-quart (1½ to 2-L) baking dish and melt in the oven while the oven heats.

Once the butter has melted, swirl it around in the baking dish so it coats the sides, then pour it into the bowl of flour mixture. In a small bowl, whisk together the milk and egg, then add to the batter and whisk to combine. Immediately transfer the batter to the warm buttery baking dish, and pour the macerated juicy fruit all over the top.

Bake until golden brown and puffed, about 30 minutes. Serve with a spoon while hot, with vanilla ice cream or whipped cream alongside.

ORANGE SUNSHINE CAKE

1 large navel orange (12 ounces/340 g)

Nonstick cooking spray or neutral oil such as sunflower, safflower, or grapeseed, for pan

1½ cups (300 g) granulated sugar

6 large eggs

2¼ cups (232 g) almond flour

2 teaspoons grated fresh ginger

1 teaspoon kosher salt

1 teaspoon baking powder

½ teaspoon ground turmeric

Powdered sugar, for serving (optional)

MAKES ONE 9-INCH (23-CM) CAKE; SERVES 8 TO 10

What happens when you simmer an orange in a pot of water for 2 hours is a delightful kind of kitchen magic. I learned this trick from a Nigella Lawson recipe in which she simmers clementines to puree into an almond cake. Turns out it works with any kind of citrus, and orange is my favorite. I add fresh ginger and turmeric to mine to give it warm spice and a golden glow. This is a very moist cake, like a pudding you can hold in your hand, and as long as you've got a few hours and a food processor, it's one of the easiest cakes you'll ever bake, and one of the most impressive transformations your oven will give you.

In a small pot, cover your orange in water and bring to a boil over high heat. Reduce the heat and let simmer for 2 hours, until the orange is quite mushy but still holds its shape. Remove from the water and let cool. This can be done up to 2 days in advance. Chill the orange until ready to use.

Preheat the oven to 325°F (165°C).

Line a 9-inch (23-cm) pan with parchment and grease all sides with cooking spray or oil.

Puree the orange in a food processor with the sugar until smooth. Add the eggs, almond flour, ginger, salt, baking powder, and turmeric and puree until smooth. Transfer to the prepared pan.

Bake until the top of the cake is lightly golden brown and springs back when touched, 45 to 50 minutes. Slide a paring knife gently around the edges of the cake to release it from the sides, then let cool completely in the pan. Invert onto a flat plate, then invert again onto a serving plate. Sprinkle with powdered sugar if desired.

The cake keeps for up to 2 days, covered at room temperature.

HAZELNUT-BUCKWHEAT SPICE CAKE

¼ cup (55 g) unsalted
butter, melted and cooled
slightly, plus more for pan

4 large eggs

½ cup (100 g) granulated
sugar

¾ cup (165 g) packed light
brown sugar

1½ cups (130 g) hazelnut
flour (or 130 g hazelnuts,
finely ground in a food
processor)

½ cup (78 g) buckwheat flour

2 teaspoons ground
cinnamon

1½ teaspoons baking powder

1 teaspoon kosher salt

½ teaspoon ground
cardamom

½ teaspoon freshly ground
black pepper

¼ teaspoon freshly ground
nutmeg

1 teaspoon vanilla extract

Powdered sugar, for topping

MAKES ONE 9-INCH (23-CM)
CAKE; SERVES 8 TO 10

Dense, moist, and richly spiced, this is definitely a cake for colder times of the year. I love the way buckwheat flour and hazelnuts play together to give it a comfortingly earthy and totally not too sweet flavor. With whipped cream and a glass of amaro, it's a cozy end to any dinner party. A few clementines or oranges on the table would not be amiss alongside. Leftovers are excellent for breakfast or afternoon tea, and you may want to just go ahead and make this one to have out for snacking, no dinner required.

Preheat the oven to 350°F (175°C). Line the bottom of a 9-inch (23-cm) cake pan with parchment, and butter the parchment and sides of the pan.

In the bowl of a stand mixer fitted with the whisk attachment, or in a large bowl with a handheld mixer on high speed, whisk the eggs and both sugars until tripled in volume, about 6 minutes. Make sure the mixture really does triple in volume—the fluffy structure that this creates is the secret to holding this gluten-free cake together.

Meanwhile, in a medium bowl, whisk the hazelnut flour, buckwheat flour, cinnamon, baking powder, salt, cardamom, pepper, and nutmeg together and set aside.

Add the melted butter and vanilla to the egg mixture and whisk to combine. Working in three batches, whisk the dry ingredients into the wet with the mixer on the lowest possible setting until just combined. Transfer the batter to the prepared cake pan, put in the oven, and bake until the top of the cake springs back when gently poked with a finger, about 30 minutes.

Let the cake rest in the pan until cool enough to touch, then invert out of the pan onto a plate and invert again onto a cooling rack to cool completely. You don't want the top of the cake to touch the cooling rack, because it'll make an unsightly grid pattern on the top of your cake.

Just before serving, put a little bit of powdered sugar in a small sieve and tap over the top of the cake for a pretty snowfall decoration. If you'd like to get fancy, cut out a paper heart or star to place on top of the cake before tapping sugar over it, then carefully remove the paper and—voila! You've got a nice design on top.

The cake keeps for up to 5 days, covered at room temperature.

BROWN BUTTER MOCHI CAKE WITH COCONUT CRUST

6 tablespoons (90 ml) unsalted butter, plus more for pan

⅔ cup (55 g) unsweetened shredded coconut, divided

1 (13.5-ounce/400-ml) can unsweetened full-fat coconut milk

1½ cups (300 g) granulated sugar

2 large eggs

1 tablespoon vanilla extract

2¼ cups (370 g) glutinous rice flour, preferably Koda Farms Blue Star Mochiko

1 teaspoon baking powder

1 teaspoon kosher salt

MAKES ONE 9-INCH (23-CM) CAKE; SERVES 8 TO 10

The gooey-chewy coconut-sweet Hawaiian treat Butter Mochi is hard to compete with. In this take on it, I add a shredded coconut crust for extra crunch and chew, and brown the butter for a rich nutty flavor that complements the toasted coconut. If you'd like to make it dairy free, swap the butter for coconut oil and skip browning it—it works just as well, and the coconut flavor will intensify beautifully.

Preheat the oven to 350°F (175°C). Generously butter a 9-inch (23-cm) cake pan. Generously coat the pan with shredded coconut, tapping out the excess (about ⅓ cup/27 g should do it).

In a large skillet, melt the butter over medium heat. Cook, swirling often, until the butter foams and then stops foaming, smells richly nutty, and is starting to turn golden brown. Remove from the heat, pour in the coconut milk, and stir to combine, being sure to scrape up any browned bits from the bottom of the pan as you stir. Transfer to a mixing bowl. Whisk in the sugar and continue whisking until the mixture has cooled to room temperature. Add the eggs, vanilla, rice flour, baking powder, and salt and whisk until the batter is smooth.

Transfer the batter to the prepared cake pan, then evenly sprinkle the top with the remaining shredded coconut.

Bake until the top begins to crack and the cake springs back when gently pressed, 55 to 65 minutes. Transfer to a wire rack and let the cake cool in the pan for about 10 minutes. Run a knife around the perimeter of the cake, place a plate over the pan, and invert the cake onto the plate. Hold the wire rack over the cake and invert the cake again onto the rack. This tricky-sounding but easily executed maneuver helps save your pretty coconut-top crust from breakage.

The cake keeps up to 5 days, covered at room temperature.

CRÈME BRÛLÉE, THREE WAYS

1 vanilla bean

4 cups (960 ml) heavy cream

8 large egg yolks

½ cup (100 g) granulated
  sugar, plus more for
  topping

¼ teaspoon kosher salt

SERVES 8, RECIPE EASILY
HALVED TO SERVE 4

Crème brûlée is my all-time favorite dessert, and the dessert I made for the very first dinner party I hosted in high school. Since then, I've made it countless times and in countless ways. I will always love the classic way best of all, but chocolate crème brûlée is very good too, and a little less sweet and more intense. Another favorite way, not to be limited to the holiday season, is to flavor it like eggnog with warm baking spices and brandy. However you make it, you need a torch to get that hard sugar crust on top, which is after all the raison d'être of crème brûlée. A basic hardware store propane torch will do just fine, but I like the convenience (and safety!) of a small handheld butane kitchen torch that I can wield right at the dining table.

1. CLASSIC CRÈME BRÛLÉE

Preheat the oven to 325°F (165°C) and set a kettle of water to boil.

Slice the vanilla bean in half and scrape the seeds out into a medium pot. Add the vanilla bean halves and the cream, then bring to a simmer over medium heat. Remove from the heat and let sit for 10 minutes to infuse the flavor of the vanilla into the cream. Fish out the vanilla bean halves, rinse, and let dry to save for another use, such as adding to a bowl of sugar for vanilla-scented sugar, or adding to your next pot of hot cocoa.

In a large, preferably spouted, mixing bowl, whisk together the egg yolks, sugar, and salt. Grab a buddy if there's someone around, and have them slowly stream the hot infused cream into the egg mixture while you whisk constantly. If you are alone, use a spouted measuring cup to pour the hot cream in bit by bit with one hand while you whisk with the other. Adding the hot cream to the egg mixture slowly ensures that bits of the egg don't cook on contact, and it eliminates the need to strain the custard before baking, which is a total bother. Use a rubber spatula to make sure you scrape all the vanilla seeds out of the pot into your egg mixture—that's the good stuff!

Arrange eight 8-ounce (225-g) ramekins in a baking dish or roasting pan. If you don't have a dish or pan big enough, use two. Divide the custard mixture among the ramekins. (This is where a pour-spout bowl comes in handy, but you can also use a ladle or a measuring cup.) Place on the center rack of the oven, then pour the boiled water from the kettle around the ramekins so that it comes halfway up their sides. You could, of course, pour the hot water in before you put it in the oven if you're feeling brave. Please don't try to make your custard mixture in advance of baking it—it needs to still be warm when it goes into the oven to help it cook evenly.

Bake until the custards are just set, 25 to 35 minutes, depending on the depth of your ramekins. They should still jiggle slightly when you tap the edge of a ramekin, but not

slosh. Let cool in the water bath slightly, then very carefully remove each ramekin onto a tray or rimmed baking dish and let cool to room temperature. Cover with plastic or a clean dish towel, being sure not to let the cover touch the surface of the custards, and chill in the fridge or in a cold but not freezing enclosed garage or porch (below 40°F [4.5°C] and above 32°F [0°C]) for at least 4 hours or overnight.

Just before serving, top each custard with about one teaspoon of sugar, gently rotating the ramekin to evenly coat the top, adding more if needed. Use a blowtorch to caramelize the sugar, moving the flame quickly around in circles to evenly cook the surface. You want the sugar to get dark brown but not black, so don't hold the torch too close to the sugar. It can take a few times to get this right, but don't worry, it still tastes good if it burns in areas. Let it cool for a few seconds, then run a finger over the top to make sure the crust is hard. If it's not, you need to add more sugar and torch it some more. I have a small handheld kitchen torch whose flame is small enough to feel safe to use at the dinner table, so I pass around sugar-topped custards for my guests to brûlée for themselves, and it adds a literal *flare* of fun to dessert. Eat them while they're hot, cracking the hard sugar crust with the back of your spoon—my favorite moment.

2. CHOCOLATE CRÈME BRÛLÉE

Add 4 ounces (115 g) finely chopped bittersweet or semisweet chocolate to the pot with the vanilla and cream and stir often to melt the chocolate as it heats. Reduce the sugar in the egg mixture to ¼ cup (50 g), and proceed with the rest of the recipe as written.

3. EGGNOG CRÈME BRÛLÉE

Add 2 cinnamon sticks, 2 cloves, ½ teaspoon freshly grated nutmeg, and 1 tablespoon brandy or bourbon to the pot with the vanilla and cream and proceed with the rest of the recipe as written.

BERRY-TAHINI SEMIFREDDO

For the berry swirl

2 cups (10 ounces/280 g) wild blueberries, blackberries, raspberries, or sliced strawberries

2 tablespoons granulated sugar

1 tablespoon sherry or red wine vinegar

½ teaspoon freshly ground black pepper

For the semifreddo

5 egg yolks

½ cup (100 g) granulated sugar

1 teaspoon kosher salt

½ cup (120 ml) tahini

2 cups (480 ml) heavy cream

SERVES 8 TO 10

I believe in leaving the ice cream making to the ice cream professionals—they have the equipment and skills to make it better than I ever can. So, when it's hot and a frozen dessert is what I want to make, semifreddo is the name of my game, no special equipment required. This frozen dessert slices like a cake to reveal streaks of tart berry swirl through a creamy frozen tahini confection. (We can't call it ice cream, but it sure tastes kind of like it.) Michael Solomonov, chef-owner of Zahav in Philadelphia, has long had a tahini semifreddo on his menu that I've dreamed of but never tried, so it's thanks to him that I decided to stir tahini into my favorite easy frozen dessert. And a good thing too—not only does the sesame paste add heavenly flavor, but it also helps prevent the dessert from getting too icy.

MAKE THE BERRY SWIRL

In a medium pot, bring the berries, sugar, vinegar, and pepper to a boil over medium heat. Cook, stirring occasionally and mashing the berries with the back of a spoon, until thickened into a sauce, 6 to 8 minutes. Transfer to a bowl and chill until fully cooled, about 30 minutes.

MAKE THE SEMIFREDDO

Line a loaf pan with plastic wrap, overhanging on all sides, and set a pot of water over medium heat to simmer.

In a large heat-proof bowl, place the egg yolks, sugar, and salt and set over the pot of simmering water. Whisk constantly until you can no longer feel sugar granules between your fingers, 2 to 4 minutes. Remove from the heat and immediately whisk in the tahini. It will be thick and gloopy, but try to get it as smooth as you can. Set aside.

In the bowl of a stand mixer fitted with the whisk attachment or in a large mixing bowl with a large whisk, whisk the heavy cream until stiff peaks form.

Whisk a quarter of the whipped cream into the tahini-egg mixture to lighten it. Using a rubber spatula, fold half of the remaining whipped cream into the tahini-egg mixture, then fold in the rest. Transfer to the prepared loaf pan.

Dollop the chilled berry mixture over the top of the tahini-egg mixture, then use a knife to swirl it into the mixture by inserting the knife almost all the way to the bottom then dragging the knife in a zig-zag pattern once back and forth and once

side to side across the pan. Pull the plastic up over the top and freeze until firm, at least 8 hours and up to 2 days.

Before serving, pull the semifreddo out of the pan by the overhang of plastic wrap and invert it onto a cutting board, discarding the wrap. If it's frozen stuck, fill a large bowl or baking dish with hot water and float the loaf pan in it for a minute, being careful not to get any water in the semifreddo, then try to invert again. Slice the loaf crosswise and serve.

AMARO-CHOCOLATE CLOUD CAKE

¾ cup (170 g) unsalted
butter, cut into pieces,
plus more for pan

1 cup (200 g) granulated
sugar, divided, plus more
for pan

8 ounces (225 g) best-quality
bittersweet chocolate,
coarsely chopped

5 large eggs, separated, at
room temperature

2 tablespoons amaro (or
brandy or vanilla extract)

1 teaspoon kosher salt

MAKES ONE 9-INCH (23-CM)
CAKE; SERVES 8 TO 10

A signature recipe of the late Richard Sax, chocolate cloud cake is a flourless chocolate cake made with separated eggs so that the cake billows and puffs and collapses like a cloud. My version is a little simpler than the classic, and a little denser. This is my go-to birthday cake, and I like to flavor mine with a shot of amaro, which lends a pleasantly haunting whisper of bitter spice to the chocolate flavor. If amaro is not your thing, or you don't have any in stock, try brandy instead, or swap in vanilla extract for a milder, classic flavor.

Preheat the oven to 350°F (175°C) with a rack in the center. Line the bottom of a 9-inch (23-cm) springform pan with parchment paper. Butter and sugar the sides of the pan. Set a pot of water over medium heat to simmer.

Place the chocolate in a heatproof bowl set over but not touching the gently simmering water on the stove. Stir the chocolate occasionally with a rubber spatula until it's fully melted, then remove the bowl from the heat and stir in the butter until smooth.

Whisk the egg yolks with ½ cup (100 g) of the sugar just until combined. Slowly whisk in the warm chocolate mixture. Whisk in the amaro and salt.

In the bowl of a stand mixer, beat the egg whites until foamy, about 2 minutes. Gradually add the remaining ½ cup (100 g) sugar and beat until glossy, soft peaks form that hold their shape but aren't quite stiff, about 5 minutes more. Very gently fold about a quarter of the beaten egg whites into the chocolate mixture to lighten it, then gently fold in the remaining whites. Scrape the batter into the prepared pan and smooth the top.

Set the springform pan on a sheet pan and bake until the top is puffed and cracked, and the center is no longer wobbly, 30 to 40 minutes. Be careful not to bake the cake beyond this point.

Let the cake cool in the pan on a rack. The center of the cake will sink as it cools, forming a sort of crater—this is good! Let the cake cool completely on a rack.

AFTER-DINNER (OR DESSERT) DRINKS

The end of dinner does not have to mean the end of a dinner party. Nor does the end of dessert. There's more chatting, games, dishes, dancing, and/or sing-alongs to do. All of these activities can be encouraged by after-dinner drinks. Just don't forget to keep serving water too, and don't let anyone drive a car if they've over-imbibed! Putting out an after-dinner drinks station symbolizes your desire to have your guests stay as late into the night as they like. (If, for any reason, you actually *do* want your guests to leave after dessert, don't do this.) Friends who have stayed at a dinner party past 2 AM like to say that my home is a time warp. I couldn't think of a better compliment in the world, and I'm honored to receive it. I usually set out the after-dinner drinks during dessert, in the center of the table for easy reach. And then when we move to the living room, I bring them with us.

DIGESTIFS

This is my go-to move: I fill one of my ice buckets (see, I told you I use them) with ice, grab my ice tongs (another nonessential hosting upgrade), and plop it on the table. Next comes as many fancy little glasses as there are guests (or I skip this and let them use their wine glasses) and a couple bottles of digestifs. Digestifs are traditionally bittersweet, herbal infused liqueurs, and practically every country has their own version, but I'm a little more expansive as to what counts as an after-dinner drink at my table. My go-tos are a bottle of amaro (I love Forthave Spirits Marseille Amaro from Brooklyn or Nonino from Italy) and a bottle of nice whiskey (my current favorite is the New York–made Excelsior bourbon). If they want to partake, guests can pour themselves a little splash of one or the other and add an ice cube. Sometimes I just serve amaro. Sometimes I have another

fun bottle to offer, like blackcurrant liqueur (the one made by Currant is fantastic), or my favorite Czech digestif Becherovka, or a second type of amaro or a cognac. (For what it's worth, a bottle of amaro is my favorite host gift to give *and* receive.)

DESSERT WINE

For a lower alcohol-by-volume after-dinner drink (either in addition to any of the digestif options above or instead of), choose a dessert wine. I will always love a cup of Portuguese tawny port (over ice for me) with cake. Or, a glass of amontillado or oloroso sherry can be the perfect slightly sweet and nutty drink to pair with dessert. Syrupy Pedro Ximenez sherry is just too thick and sweet for me, but some people like that. For a chilled and bubbly dessert pairing, a bottle of the sweet, sparkling Italian wine Moscato d'Asti is a festive treat. Talk to your local wine shop if you're interested in trying more

different dessert wines from around the world. After dessert is done, if I want to keep serving wine, I'll put out a light and dry sparkling wine because I often want a refreshing cold thing after all the eating is done. But be sure to keep some red wine out on the table too, because there will be plenty who prefer to stick with red—now's the time for lighter reds though, not so much the time for a rich and deeply tannic red.

COFFEE AND TEA

For those not drinking alcohol (and even for those who are), offer to make coffee or herbal tea. Some guests (like my father) like coffee with their dessert no matter what, so it's always a good idea to be ready to brew a pot. Prep your coffee before guests arrive if you can, so that all you have to do is push the start button on your pot as you put out dessert.

SOURCES

A few of my favorite places to buy ingredients, kitchen tools, and tabletop treasures on the internet.

INGREDIENTS

Burlap & Barrel

All my favorite spices as well as chile flakes and kelp flakes, all equitably sourced.

burlapandbarrel.com

King Arthur

Flours and specialty baking ingredients, and the source of my go-to gluten-free all-purpose flour.

shop.kingarthurbaking.com

Bob's Red Mill

The best almond flour, hazelnut flour, polenta, oats, and more!

bobsredmill.com

Thrive Market

Organic pantry staples (flaky sea salt! olive oil! coconut milk! tahini! chocolate! fish sauce! tamari!) in the mail at a discount (with membership).

thrivemarket.com

Rancho Gordo

The very best heirloom beans.

ranchogordo.com

Rancho Meladuco Date Farm

The softest, freshest, most delicious California dates ever.

ranchomeladuco.com

Kingston Wine Co.

My favorite local wine shop where I live focuses on biodynamic, organic, and natural wines from all around the world. I love everything they sell, and I am always learning from them. They have a great website and ship (almost) everywhere.

kingstonwine.com

Wine + Peace

Sustainably made American wines from small producers. Their site is easy to use, educational, and full of new discoveries. They ship (almost) everywhere.

wineandpeace.com

KITCHEN AND TABLETOP

Etsy

I spend way too much time scrolling through Etsy, but it's where many of my dishes, glasses, and flatware that you see in this book came from, and it's always a rewarding treasure hunt. The best source for platters on the internet.

etsy.com

Food52

A well-curated selection of cooking tools and equipment as well as lovely tableware, linens, and candles.

food52.com/shop

Coming Soon

Whimsical, modern, and completely irresistible glassware, utensils, and more fun items for the table and home.

comingsoonnewyork.com

Felt + Fat

Colorful creamy-coated ceramics and platters hand made in Philadelphia.

feltandfat.com

Concrete Cat

Canadian concrete design atelier, makers of my favorite lazy Susan/ serving platter.

concretecat.com

Fable New York

Gorgeous and unbreakable bamboo dishes for kids, patios, picnics, and everyday use.

fableny.com

Hawkins New York

So many beautiful things for the kitchen, table, and home.

hawkinsnewyork.com

Bennington Potters

Handmade stoneware platters, bowls, baking dishes, plates, and more from Vermont.

benningtonpotters.com

OXO

The world's greatest cooking tongs, angled measuring cups, food storage containers, and more.

oxo.com

AFTER A DINNER PARTY

And so here we are at the end of all the menus and advice I've collected in my life of hosting dinner parties thus far. I hope it's useful to you. More than anything, I hope it brings you joy, and some meaningful connections. I started writing this book before a global pandemic, but I finished writing it during one, home alone with my cats dreaming of the day when I could gather friends and lovers around my table again. That day took too long to come, and now that it's here, I hope I never take being able to gather for granted again. Every dinner party, no matter the size, occasion, or even the food that is served, is special simply because it brings a group of different people together to share, for a moment, the most basic ritual of life: nourishment. I hope you feel ready to host some dinner parties now, and I hope you won't sweat the small stuff. Let your guests help you with a load of dishes after dessert then leave the wine glasses and serving platters until morning, and spend the last hours of your night (or into the early morning) dancing or talking instead of cleaning. I love waking up to signs that a party happened in my house last night: empty glasses and bottles reflecting sunlight across the table, stains on the tablecloth, napkins hungover in disarray. Look, something good happened here! Brew some coffee, turn up the oldies, and clean that beautiful mess slowly as you remember the highlights of the night before.

With love,
Anna

INDEX

ACKNOWLEDGMENTS

Thank you to my agent, Adriana Stimola, for convincing me that yes, it was time to write this book, and for fighting for my vision and cheering me on throughout the whole long process. I can't believe we finally did the thing we dreamed of doing when we first met so many years ago; I never could have done it without you.

To the team at Abrams, especially to my ever-patient editor Laura Dozier, thank you for believing in my vision and turning it into a book. And thank you Lizzie Allen for designing that book to match my vision.

To Chelsea Kyle, thank you for wanting to make the photographs for my book with me. You are a wizard who can intuit the contents of my brain and turn them into pictures that look even better than I'd ever imagined. And to Gabrielle Lakshmi, who joined our covid-safe photo team and made every shoot day easier and more fun, and whose hands and face now grace the pages of this book. And to the Copeland-Gipp family, Julian Focareta, Nicole Bergen, and Theo Hunt, who showed up to sit around my table and have their pictures taken too, thank you for making this book look more like the party it's meant to be.

To Kat Boytsova, who always makes me a better cook when she's around. Thank you for all the recipe brainstorming, testing, problem-solving, and food styling assistance for the past six plus years, but especially for this book: My recipes work better and look better because of you.

To David Tamarkin, for being my biggest career cheerleader and favorite editor: I'm forever grateful. And to all my other former Condé Nast coworkers and test kitchen family: thank you for making me a better cook, eater, writer, and stylist. Thank you especially to Rhoda Boone, for teaching me how to be a real food stylist, and a better recipe writer.

To Jesse Sparks, thank you for being an extra set of careful eyes on the manuscript. And to Mike Soto, for always being there to help clarify my thoughts and written words. And to my sweet cats, Francis and Felix, for keeping me company through all the late nights of writing this book.

To all the friends and lovers who have joined me for dinner parties around my table throughout the years, thank you for making me a better host and a better cook. To my constant dinner party guests since high school Hillary and Michaela, thank you for knowing me so well for so long and always loving me. To my most loyal Brooklyn dinner party partners in crime Patrick and Julia and Pete and Carola, thank you for believing that this thing I've always loved to do was worthy of a book, and for brainstorming with me and cheering me on throughout the process of turning it into one. And to my love Jack, for supporting me while I finished this book, and for making my weeknight dinner table into a place of rituals and sharing again.

And last but not least, to my family. To my Mama, who taught me how to cook as a child, but more importantly how to cook by feeling and mood and with intuition and passion. Thank you for filling our house with cookbooks and food magazines—I always loved looking at them, but never dreamed I'd get to make them! To my Pops, who always does the dishes no matter how big of a mess we make in the kitchen, and who taught me the importance of rituals, candlelight, and occasional tears at the dinner table. And to my sisters, who are still my favorite sous chefs, thank you for testing so many of the recipes in this book, and for eating so many of my experiments over the years. And to my whole Mustin family, whose love for trying and cooking new food was contagious, and who showed me from an early age that lingering around the table is an event in itself.

ANNA STOCKWELL is a food stylist and editor who was most recently a senior food editor for Epicurious and *Bon Appétit*. While at Epicurious, Stockwell hosted a popular weekly Instagram story called *At Home With Anna*. She has also worked at *Saveur* and has experience cooking in the test kitchens for *Every Day With Rachael Ray* and *Real Simple*. Stockwell holds a degree in classic culinary arts from the International Culinary Center, and her video series *No Recipe Required* was nominated for a James Beard Award. She lives in New York's Hudson Valley.

Editor: Laura Dozier
Managing Editor: Glenn Ramirez
Design Manager: Danny Maloney
Production Manager: Alison Gervais

Book design by Lizzie Allen

Library of Congress Control Number: 2021946809

ISBN: 978-1-4197-5144-8
eISBN: 978-1-64700-689-1

Printed and bound in the United States
10 9 8 7 6 5 4 3 2 1

Abrams books are available at special discounts when
purchased in quantity for premiums and promotions as well
as fundraising or educational use. Special editions can also
be created to specification. For details, contact specialsales@
abramsbooks.com or the address below.

Abrams® is a registered trademark of Harry N. Abrams, Inc.

ABRAMS The Art of Books
195 Broadway, New York, NY 10007
abramsbooks.com